SAVING MYSELF

ONE STEP

AT A TIME

SAVING MYSELF ONE STEP AT A TIME

A RUNNING MEMOIR

T. J. BRYAN

LOCUST TREE PUBLISHING

Copyright © 2020 by Thelma Jane Bryan

All rights reserved.

ISBN: 978-0-578-76894-6

1. Biography and memoir—Sports 2. Biography and memoir—Running 3. Biography and memoir—Women runners 4. Biography and memoir—Aging runners 5. Biography and memoir—African-American runners 6. Biography and memoir—African-American women runners 7. Biography and memoir—Running to relieve anxiety, depression, despair, and stress

Disclaimers

This memoir contains the author's recollections of past experiences. Some names and characteristics have been changed, some events have been compressed, and most dialogue has been recreated.

This book contains information about running injuries and treatments. Such content is not intended as a substitute for professional medical advice, diagnosis, or treatment. The reader should consult a physician about any symptoms that may require medical attention.

Cover Photo: T. J. Bryan Crossing the Finish Line of the 2011 Boston Marathon

DEDICATION

To the woman whose strength has inspired me over a lifetime—my Mama, Mary G. Bryan,

and

to my closest friends—David G. Preston, my stalwart husband and faithful one-man racing crew, and Bryan D. Preston, our son and my role model for kindness

CONTENTS

Preface 1

Joy: My First Boston Marathon 6

Despair: Life Without Purpose 9

Persistence: Rookie Runner 16

Childhood Fears: Fleeing from Monsters 22

Non-Stop Humiliation: No Matter the Game 28

Braving Aerobics Classes 33

Grudging Move to a New Home 39

Apprehension: Joining a Running Club 43

Too Much of a Good Thing: Races, Races, Races 54

Determination: A Post-Exhaustion Return to Running 60

A Would-Be Predator in a Car 63

Invoking Mama's Inner Toughness (My First Marathon) 66

Encounters of the Surreal Kind: Training for the 2011 Boston Marathon 72

Halcyon Days: My Third, Fourth, and Fifth Marathons 78

A Grateful Return to Racing: My Sixth Marathon 87

A Move to an Almost Perfect Running Setting 94

Bird Phobia, Begone! 97

The Loneliness of Solo Running 99

Constant Threats: Dogs, Dogs, Dogs 106

Trail Creatures Abounding: Gnats, Cats, Rodents, a Fox, and a Bear 115

Good Vibes from Most Trail People 120

Horror: Confederate Flags near the Trail 128

Fear on the Trail: To Arm or Not to Arm 132
Running Woes: Tinkling, Nausea, and Trots 136
Battling Insomnia and Rarely Winning 143
Debacle: The 2016 Boston Marathon
(My Seventh Marathon) 148
Starstruck: Encounters with Running Superstars 159
Self-Deprecation and the Need to Redeem Myself 163
Fitting in Immediately: An Additional Running Club 167
A Grind: Winter Marathon Training 177
Good Fortune: My Eighth Marathon 184
Impulsively Joining an Online Running Group 186
Ouch! A Run-Stopping Injury 188
Carefully Preparing for the 2018 Boston Marathon 192
Badass Running: The 2018 Boston Marathon
(My Ninth Marathon) 195
Yet Another Injury 209
Mistakes and Heat Exhaustion: Preparing for My
Tenth Marathon 216
Pragmatism: My Tenth Marathon 227
Oh, Happy Day! Another Morning Run 235
Acknowledgments 238
One Last Thing 240

PREFACE

I am an anomaly. A former university chancellor and an African-American woman now in her mid-70s, I became a runner in 2009, when I was 64 years old. I was an unlikely person to begin such a journey. Throughout most of my life, sports did not interest me. Although I participated in aerobics during the 1980s and 1990s, I had exhibited little athletic talent or ability otherwise. Initially, running was a distraction from the ruins of my professional life.

When I lost my chancellorship, I reminded myself that I had come back from challenges in the past. As a young child, I was so seriously ill that I was in a coma and could not walk when I awakened. In my 50s, I was ambushed by cancer, but I rebounded and went on with my life. This time, though, the challenge was radically different. My perennially tenuous sense of self-worth was at stake.

What I learned in six months or so after I became a runner was that I was fast enough to win age-group awards at a range of distances in local races. Over time, I embraced the full marathon (26.2 miles), many runners' least favorite distance, no doubt because of its toll on the mind and body. From 2009 to 2019, I competed in ten marathons. I qualified for the Holy Grail of distance running, the Boston Marathon, in eight of these races. I ran in this prestigious race three times. Initially, I planned to run only once but could not overcome the lure of returning twice more.

As a woman marathoner in her 70s, I belong to a select group. Only .2 percent of females who finished worldwide marathons in

2019 were in this age group. A much smaller percentage of such runners were African-American women.

I have continued to run because the sport has given me far more than I anticipated. Membership in a new community I expected. The meditation during runs that led to my seeing myself more honestly I did not expect. Understanding that every step leads to self-salvation I did not anticipate. These unexpected benefits have come to me almost exclusively outdoors as I experienced nature's bounty—fresh air flowing, clear streams gleaming, gray rocks jutting, green vegetation in spring and summer and orange and brown in fall and winter embracing me, and woodland creatures flying or scampering. In this world, I keep anguish at bay.

I do not take running for granted. I have been sidelined by injuries and have had to go on hiatuses, but, repeatedly, I return to the sport after recovering. I have been frightened by media accounts that remind me of my vulnerability as a female solo runner, but I swallow my fear and run alone nonetheless when I must. I have encountered symbols of racial animosity, but I run on after overcoming shock followed by anger and sorrow. I love and need the sport so much that nothing is going to stop me as long as I remain healthy enough to run.

Readily, I acknowledge that running may not appeal to others. My son, who is a weight lifter and a power walker, tells me often when I proselytize, "Mom, I don't like running." While I want to nag or cajole him, I yield the field. Finding a sport that gives satisfaction and respite from woe is a personal matter.

While I hope this memoir appeals to runners, I also hope it interests fitness athletes who pursue swimming, yoga, seated and standing aerobics, and a variety of other sports.

Additionally, I hope it appeals to a variety of other readers: to anyone whose life has been turned upside down and who has found ways to overcome self-doubt and dismay, to anyone who has pondered a leap into fitness but has not moved from thought to action, to anyone who welcomes reassurance that she or he can begin or continue fitness activities as aging occurs, and to anyone who may draw sustenance from the accomplishments of someone who has persisted in a sport against the odds.

SAVING MYSELF ONE STEP

AT A TIME

A RUNNING MEMOIR

Joy: My First Boston Marathon

I was almost 64 years old when I became a runner.

Two years later, when I was three months shy of my 66th birthday, I counted the minutes before I would line up to begin the 2011 Boston Marathon, my second-ever 26.2-mile race. This was one of the most prestigious marathons in the entire world. That I was competing was beyond my wildest imagination.

The weather conditions were ideal. The temperature hovered around the mid-40s. The humidity was low. Tailwinds were predicted and would likely push runners toward the finish line. These conditions portended fast finishing times for racers.

In the athletes' village, a sprawling dirt field in Hopkinton, Massachusetts, I sat alone on a large black lawn-and-leaf trash bag that I had placed on the ground, which was punctuated with patches of scraggly browning grass beaten down by countless feet. A brunette woman who appeared to be in her early twenties sat on the ground about six feet away from me. Slowly, she drained the contents of a can of 5-hour ENERGY.

I was supposed to be forcing myself into a zone, so I blocked out this runner. Shutting out not only her but every other woman and man in the milling crowd, I waited for my group, the slowest runners, to walk to the starting line. Once we began to move in this direction, I stayed at the back of the pack. In this position, I would not be tempted to run too fast and deplete my energy too soon. I would run a tad faster after the first five miles or so. Gradually, I would increase my speed during the remaining distance.

Thud. Thud. Thud. Thud. Thud. Thud. Thud. Thud. I adjusted the impact of my feet as they pounded the asphalt during the first mile. I reminded myself to land lightly and to pretend I was running on hot coals.

Patter. Patter. Patter. Patter. Patter. Patter. Patter. Patter. That's better. Not as much energy going into the ground and thus wasted.

The first few miles were downhill. I took advantage of gravity, relaxed, and let my body float. I gave my arms a break. No point in pumping them as I descended. No strength running until I was on an uphill or on flats.

Around the marathon's halfway point, the roar of the Scream Tunnel, the area in which Wellesley-College students and other spectators cheered and applauded as runners passed, broke through my zone. I sealed the space again. I heard nothing. About seven miles later, I ascended Heartbreak Hill, recognizable to me only when I happened to look down to see the name of this historic location spray painted on the asphalt.

Giggling children bounced along on the sides of the course. Hoping for high fives and hand slaps, some leaned toward us runners as we passed. I succumbed to the youngsters' enthusiasm. Repeatedly, I ran toward the edges of the course, extended one of my hands, positioning it so that the children's sticky hands met my palm for a second. I thought that this would be my first and last Boston Marathon. Why not have a good time?

On this day, Kenyan runner Geoffrey Mutai electrified the road-racing world when he crossed the finish line in Boston in two hours, three minutes, and two seconds (2:03:02)—a course record. Mutai's countrywoman Caroline Kilel and US runner Desiree Davila dueled during the final yards for first place among the women. Like many other spectators, my patriotic husband David alternated, he told me later, between loudly screaming and silently, but fervently, praying as he jumped up and down and clapped his hands raw in an effort to will Davila to victory. Alas! Kilel broke the tape in 2:22:36. Davila trailed the Kenyan by two seconds.

A little more than two hours later, David still stood in virtually the same space. As soon as I saw the finish line, I spotted his slightly flushed face and gleaming, fluffy silver hair, the latter distinctive even at a distance. Relief and a quiet smile were his responses to my arrival.

I crossed the line in 4:25:58. I was tenth of 45 women in my age group (65-69 years old). I was one of almost 24,000 finishers and one of more than 10,000 women finishers. As far as I could tell, I was one of a relatively small number of African-American women in the race.

Despair: Life Without Purpose

From 2003 to 2007, I served as chancellor of a historically Black public university in the Deep South. David accompanied me, joining the university's department of mathematics and computer science as an associate professor. When I was suddenly relieved of my position in July 2007, I returned northward to our Maryland home.

The loss of my chancellorship was rooted in a step I was unwilling to take early on. Shortly before my arrival, a company operated by a state legislator's wife lost the dining contract at the university after students complained to the system head about poor-quality food and unsatisfactory customer service. The lawmaker wanted me to solicit vendors when the three-year contract ended. Given that the university was not barred from staying with the current vendor and given that students were satisfied with the dining program, I would not agree to do so. In response to my refusal, a friend of the legislator threatened me during a telephone conversation. "If you don't make sure that the dining contract goes out for bids next time around, you're going to regret ever coming to this city," he yelled. When I was not malleable, the legislator and his buddies maligned me whenever opportunities arose. The woman who led the system when I was hired ignored these detractors. However, her successor heeded the attacks against me. After two years of being highly regarded, I was held in disfavor when the leadership of the system changed.

Despite this uncomfortable situation, success after success was mine. Record-setting fundraising. Saving the education program at the nearby army base when its director failed to implement federal changes. The establishment of new academic programs. The attainment of specialized accreditations denoting superior academic-program quality. Presentations galore at community luncheons, women's-group meetings, churches, and community colleges. My very own National-Public-Radio talk show highlighting university initiatives. Collaboration with the county public-school system to establish an early-college high school. An alliance with the city fire department to establish a station on campus. Partnerships with community colleges to ensure that students transferred seamlessly to the university. The creation of partnerships with Chinese universities. An outstanding performance appraisal from the university's board of trustees. And on and on.

With little warning, the new system head abruptly ripped me from my position just as a gardener might have yanked an errant weed from an otherwise pristine lawn. I might have saved myself had not two variables worked against me. The university's business office failed to implement a new software system successfully. A fledgling academic program got off to the rockiest of starts. Constantly, the newspaper in the city where the university was located published savage articles about these two issues. Additionally, my being a first—the first woman appointed by the university system board of governors to serve as chancellor of the institution—did not endear me to supporters of patriarchy. My hailing from a place other than the state was a minus at a time when there was a clamor for native daughters and sons as leaders of public universities there. My marriage to a White man did not help me. Some people in the community looked askance at my becoming the first African-American member of the local country club.

My supporters attempted to save me. Individually, members of the board of trustees beseeched the system head to reconsider. University faculty, staff, and students signed a petition and sent emails and letters of support to the system head as did some alumni and community members. All for naught.

Perhaps had I thrown the person with direct responsibility for the business unit and the person with responsibility for the academic department under the bus, I might have saved myself. I could not bring myself to take such a step, though. My downfall was in the final analysis my fault. I had trusted but had not verified.

As soon as I, caught flatfooted, realized that I was done at the university, I flagellated myself. I should have departed shortly after the removal of the former system head. I had been offered an opportunity to lead a university in another state. Loyalty to the university that I led and my belief that I was doing the right things to enhance the institution kept me where I was. This decision cost me my career. Because of the abruptness of my departure, David did not have adequate time to search for another position, so he remained behind at the university, where he continued to teach theory of computation, programming languages, and the like.

In our Maryland home, from time to time, I descended to the basement, where I came face to face with tangible evidence of my past achievements. Dust-laden cardboard boxes crammed with oak, walnut, and mahogany plaques with my name inscribed on faux-silver or faux-gold plates teetered precariously in a shaky pyramid in a corner of the storage area. In a honey-oak filing cabinet were manila folders so bursting full of appreciation certificates and outstanding-performance appraisals that their once stiff and sharp bottoms had become soft and rounded. Occasionally, a few escapees from these folders slithered out, fell behind the drawers, and caused jamming that prevented closure. Atop the filing cabinet, two urns, one ivory and one royal blue, heralded my completion of leadership-development programs. Next to them sat three cobwebby acrylic clocks with gold-tone metal plates affixed to their fronts summarizing long-forgotten contributions to nonprofit organizations benefiting women and children in need.

Such a focus of my volunteerism was natural, for I grew up excruciatingly aware of the gap between the fortunate and the unfortunate in US society. I was the daughter of working-class parents who never graduated from high school but who endured in the face of personal faults and foibles and despite the harshness of African-American life. If I preceded David in death, these recognitions would undoubtedly remain where they were. In his mind, casting them aside would be a diminution of my successes.

While my mother and father handed me no silver spoons, they did bequeath to me something of great value. They planted deeply in my soul a fervent belief in the American Dream. Since my earliest days—at home, church, and school, the constant message was that hard work would lead me down a path at whose terminus I would find prosperity and happiness.

After a lifetime of pursuing the Dream nonstop, at the age of 62, I moved through such an altered landscape that I felt trapped in a never-ending nightmare. After close to 30 years in the college and university world, the infighting, backstabbing, and maneuvering—famously described as "the most vicious and bitter form of politics, because the stakes are so low"—had drained me thoroughly. Even before my ouster, I had lost the ability to laugh when my perennially amusing son engaged in witty repartee, the ability to feel happy when my husband surprised me with flowers when no holiday or special occasion led me to expect a token of affection, and the ability to grieve when friends of many decades and relatives passed away. I could not even cry for myself when I lost my chancellorship. I had become a woman of stone. The travails of academic leadership and the concomitant need for constancy and consistency had rendered me emotionless.

As I wandered in what seemed like a wasteland, not a single day transpired when I did not think about my mother or see her image—her weary brown eyes, her caramel skin, her small pert nose, and the small thin spot in her hair at the crown of her head. One night during this dark chapter, as I surrendered to self-pity as I lay in bed, she, five years dead, wrapped me in her arms as she had rarely done during her lifetime. Providing the essentials of life to six girls born during nine years while caring for other people's girls and boys, washing and ironing other people's clothes, scrubbing other people's floors, cooking other people's meals, and coping with a husband whose fondness for whiskey exceeded his love for her left her little time to show affection to her children—even the neediest one of them. That night Mama whispered, "You shouldn't be sad because of some damned job." I responded, "I'm so ashamed." For a few seconds, she was quiet. Then she murmured, "You should be proud of yourself. You went to college and graduated in four years even though, as the second oldest of my girls, you had to hold down a full-time job at the same time. You worked because your daddy and me needed you to help us make ends meet. You got all those A grades. You earned that doctor's degree. You got all those promotions at work. You married a man who would do anything for you. You have the sweetest and smartest son in the world." She paused. Softly, she urged, "Stop feeling sorry for yourself. Thank the Lord for your blessings." Then I could no longer feel her arms.

During this period, I could not escape a sense of floundering. I was nominated for four chancellorships/presidencies, and I was invited to three interviews. I even reached a finalists' list once, but nothing came of these forays. I wondered whether I had been blacklisted. Due diligence would have dictated that my former employer be consulted. Maybe I had lost my edge. A headhunter observed after one of my interviews that I seemed fatigued. An internet search would have easily led to the venomous newspaper articles. Who knows?

Meanwhile, the woman who led the system at the beginning of my chancellorship had become the president of a national association located in Washington, DC. She offered me a position as manager of a grant program the association oversaw. This move would have been a giant step backward. I had no interest in the program's focus. Lodging in the city, professional clothing, and other items associated with employment would have consumed most of the money I would have earned. I declined the opportunity.

I felt I was on a scrap heap, where I would remain. Once a university or college leader, especially a woman, went down, historically, there was usually no getting back up, especially after her departure becomes media fodder.

I contemplated professional reinvention, but I could not fathom transformation. What would I become? What would I do? I had no idea. Purposeless, I counted the days.

In this funk, I thought about how life had blindsided me nine years earlier. From out of nowhere, in 1998, I was diagnosed with cancer in my right breast. None of the women in my family had suffered from this condition. I had been careful about my diet, and I was fit. I suffered through mammograms annually.

When I expressed bewilderment to one of my physicians, he explained that my age, then 53, increased my risk. Other than that factor, he could offer no rationale other than "bad luck." I suspected, though, that the black particles on the various desks at which I graded papers, met with students, and prepared reports for 20 years while I was a professor and administrator at a Baltimore college were the causes. Although there was never official confirmation of a relationship between the particles and my condition, this suspicion became a firmly held belief of mine when most of the women who spent significant time in the building over the years also developed breast cancer. Decades later, asbestos was removed from the building, and ventilation experts revealed that the duct work throughout the facility had been incorrectly installed.

A major illness was something I never thought would happen to me. I had taken good health for granted. Anger. Shock. Disbelief. Self-pity. Swallowing my sorrow, I fought my way back to health. Similarly, I had assumed that professional health would be mine until I decided myself to retire. Wrong twice.

PERSISTENCE: ROOKIE RUNNER

My journey as a runner began one Sunday morning in early 2009 as I leafed through the voluminous Sunday edition of *The Baltimore Sun*. Generally, I dove into the full-color comic-strip section first; scanned the entertainment section next; and skimmed through one or two articles of international, national, or regional significance last if at all. However, on this day, an article in the regional section leaped out at me and trumped my usual reading priorities. The story focused on the upcoming inaugural Maryland Half Marathon, which was scheduled on May 31, 2009. The notion of running in this race was alluring for a few seconds. Perhaps I could meet people and expand my social network. Then reality set in. I was not a runner.

Up to this point, my attention had been divided between the newspaper print and the green-and-white-speckled Corian kitchen counter. As I drank my second cup of coffee, I tried not to see the circles that testified to the numerous times that Bryan, my then 27-year-old son, and Brigitte, his then 24-year-old girlfriend, had placed dripping-wet glasses and cups on this surface during the four years when David and I lived in the Deep South. During our absence from Maryland, we had relinquished our home to our son's disregard.

I reread the newspaper article about the Maryland Half Marathon and learned that a Baltimore-area running store was providing training to prepare people for the race. The store offered prospective half marathoners an opportunity to attend a single session free of charge before making a firm commitment to participate. I took the bait. I was so naïve that I did not know that running a half marathon (13.1 miles) was hardly an optimal distance for a first-time runner.

The complimentary run occurred at a local college track that was located about 22 miles south of my home. The group was scheduled to meet around 6:30 p.m. The temperature was in the low 40s when I showed up. I wore the only fitness-related clothing that I owned—a black heavy-cotton hooded sweatshirt, a long-sleeved mousy-gray cotton t-shirt, and black cotton sweatpants. "Moisture wicking" was not yet in my lexicon.

I had read that some people believed that listening to music helped them when they ran, so I made sure I had some tunes to which I could listen. At the time, I did not own an MP3 player. I relied on my Sony-Walkman CD player. I hid it in the pouch in the front of my sweatshirt. It thumped against my pelvis with every step that I took from my car to the track.

Because I had become lost after I reached the college campus, I arrived ten minutes after the session was scheduled to begin. Once I reached the oval, I found only a fortyish woman there. Apprehensively, I asked her, "Are you here for the training session?"

She responded, "Yes, but I understand that the others are running six miles on the campus. The group didn't have permission to use the track tonight."

"Not a good sign," I said.

"We're supposed to try to catch up with the group."

"I don't have enough stamina to run to my car, which is just down the hill."

"I know what you mean. I can't run far either."

"Let's just walk around on the road until they come back."

The next morning, I drove to the running store offering the training and paid $90 for the sessions. Later in the day, I shopped in another running store for clearance-sale clothing and purchased a black pair of last season's running capris and a matching black and yellow running shirt. Next, I drove to an electronics store where I bought an MP3 player so I could listen to upbeat tunes such as Flo Rida's "Low" and Estelle's "American Boy" as I walked and ran.

With my music player clipped to my running capris' waistband, I walked onto the track a week later. Approximately 30 people were present as well as the coach, a thin thirtyish man who was also a personal trainer and competitive runner. We began that session and subsequent sessions with dynamic-movement activities designed to warm up muscles and ramp up circulation. We marched in place, we extended our legs to the front, we flexed each foot downward and then upward, we stepped from side to side, we rotated our hips in clockwise circles followed by counterclockwise circles, and we brought our heels up to our derrieres. After warming up, we ran around the track as a group. The best I could do was a slow run about one-fourth of the way around (approximately 100 meters). Then I stopped to walk a few steps. I ran again. I walked again. I ran again. I walked again. I ran again. I walked again. Two weeks would pass before I could run around the entire oval, 400 meters, without a break.

Our next session commenced on the Northern Central Railroad (NCR) Trail, a tree-lined crushed-limestone and dirt pathway popular with runners, bikers, walkers, hikers, and horseback riders. We warmed up with the coach before he opened the metaphoric corral, and we ran, or both walked and ran in my case, the prescribed miles at a pace at which we could engage in conversations if we had a companion. Silently, I communed with myself as did some of the other runners who had no one moving around the same speeds.

During the first five weeks of the training program, I progressed enough to cover four miles on the Trail in a little under an hour. Slow? Yes. But I was elated. During the final session (and tenth week), I covered ten miles for the first time.

The run consumed two and a half hours. Because of my slow speed, I formed a simple half-marathon objective: to finish the race ahead of at least one person. Given that some participants would walk the entire route and a few might not have trained adequately enough to run the entire distance, this aspiration seemed realistic.

When the half marathon launched from the edge of the Maryland State Fairgrounds, I was startled by the throng of runners. Later, I learned that more than 2,000 participated. I wore a short-sleeved gray-heather running shirt emblazoned on the front with the running store's name and the words "Half-Marathon Training Program." I did not know that the shirt screamed newbie runner until a total stranger, a twentyish woman in a sleeveless red crop top, peered at my shirt and simultaneously smiled and hissed. She said, "You're so cute." I was already self-conscious, and I loathed condescension. I imagined my nails morphing into claws that I used to shred her top.

As I waited for the race to begin, David asked me, "Why aren't you pumped? Eager?" I responded, "I don't have that luxury. To me, the race is just another day at the office." I already knew that expending emotional energy by becoming overexcited before a race was counterproductive.

Calmly and calculatingly, I ran nonstop until I reached the eleventh mile when, suddenly, David popped up on the course. He roared, "You're killing it. Keep going!" He bounced alongside me, his lustrous hair blowing in the wind. I had been in a zone until he startled me. I stopped running and started walking. What I learned later was that, at that very moment, my fuel (glycogen—carbohydrates used as an energy source during exercise) was depleted. On top of this deficit, I was inadequately hydrated. In fact, I had carried so little water that, in desperation, I drank from a bottle offered by a woman I never saw before or after the race. For me, this step was unprecedented. Historically,

I was so concerned about being infected by people's germs that Mama used to tease me because I never sipped a beverage from a container that someone else's lips—even hers—had touched.

The race ended on a dirt track where thoroughbred racing occurred during the annual Maryland State Fair. Laughing as he ran, a man trotting near me yelled, "And down the stretch they come" as a bunch of us approached the finish line. I silently vowed that this race would be my first and my last.

As I wandered around a grassy area in search of David, I spotted a muscular-looking milk-chocolate-brown woman with a long silver braid hanging from the opening in the back of her white running cap. Beautiful, she was clad in an eye-catching python-print jog bra and matching ankle-length running tights. A bevy of people encircled her. I assumed that she was a celebrity of some sort. I was surprised when I caught her eye and she smiled warmly at me. Emboldened, I slowly ran over and introduced myself. She told me her name—Ernestine. (Months later, I learned that her full name was Ernestine Shepherd and that she was listed then in the *Guinness Book of World Records* as the oldest competitive female bodybuilder in the world.)

She asked, "Did you win an award?" I confessed, "I don't know how the awards work." In response, Ernestine explained, "The fastest three men and three women regardless of their ages are overall winners." She went on to say that the fastest three men and fastest three women aged 40 or older were masters' winners and that sometimes awards were given to grandmasters (the top three men and top three women runners aged 50 or older). Additionally, age-group awards were frequently given to the fastest males and the fastest females—usually in five- or ten-year increments, she added. Because so few men and women 70 or older ran in races, often organizers did not adhere to five- or ten-year increments for this oldest group of racers. Instead, they lumped them all together into a 70-99 group. Ernestine had won the first-place award for women in the 70-99 category. I was shocked. She looked as though she might be in her 50s at the oldest.

When I checked the race results after I returned home, I learned that I had come in fourth of 12 women in the 60-64 division. My chip, or net, time (the amount of time from the second that I crossed the starting mat to the exact moment that I crossed the finish line) was 2:27:36. I ignored the column listing gun times (the amount of time between the gun start of the race and the time that I crossed the finish line). The gun time was greater than the net time unless a runner crossed the start line at precisely the same second that a race official blasted an air horn or pulled the trigger on a starter's pistol loaded with blanks. My pace, based on net time, was a middling 11:16 per mile.

At the time, I thought that chip, or net, time was used exclusively to determine placement in races. Months after my maiden race, I learned that organizers used gun time when determining overall prize winners and top overall masters and grandmasters. Some organizers also used gun time when identifying recipients of age-and-gender awards—especially in some small races when the additional cost of using chips, which had to be bought or rented, made too much of a dent in profits.

Childhood Fears: Fleeing from Monsters

One night, out of nowhere, David asked, "When you were in high school, was there a running team?"

I replied, "I don't remember any sports other than field hockey."

As a high-school student, I had neither interest nor ability in sports. Even if I had, I would not have been invited to participate. African-American girls at the school, except for one biracial girl who seemed to identify primarily with Whiteness, were made to feel unwelcome during the early 1960s when Baltimore public schools were in the early years of racial desegregation.

Memory is often unreliable, however. I pulled *The Echo 1963*, my high-school yearbook, from a bookshelf. I was jarred by the contents. Appearing on the pages of this chronicle were photographs of girls, both African American and White, participating in nine sports: archery, badminton, basketball, modern dance, softball, speedball, swimming, tennis, and volleyball. Field hockey was not one of the sports.

As I showed David the pages, he stared at me.

I said, "I was wrong."

Looking puzzled, he asked, "Wrong about what? Did you find any running activities?"

"No."

David commented, "You wouldn't have run very far back then anyway."

I knew from my reading that he was right. Limiting females' distances was par for the course before, during, and after my high-school years. The Amateur Athletic Union (AAU), the organization governing non-professional sports in the US, limited women's distance on the track to 800 meters until 1960. The organization banned women from all road races in 1961. This prohibition was not lifted until 1969. Three years later, in 1972, Title IX—which states that no person in the United States shall be excluded from participation, on the basis of sex, in any education program or activity receiving federal financial assistance—was passed. In the wake of this legislation, the AAU lifted its bans on women's distance running. A stipulation for females' participation in the marathon was that they were required to begin at a separate start line or at a separate start time from their male counterparts.

The little I knew about women in running I learned when I was elementary-school age and lived in rural Saint Mary's County, Maryland. From time to time during those years, I visited my maternal grandmother in Baltimore, and, while at her home, I read about African-American women runners when I leafed through *Jet* and *Ebony*. In these Black-oriented periodicals, I learned about Wilma Rudolph, a 100- and 200-meter sprinter who won a bronze medal during the 1956 Olympic Games.

After my family migrated to Baltimore in 1958, I had constant access to such magazines. Not only did I learn about Wilma Rudolph's subsequent three gold medals in the 1960 Olympics but also about the Tennessee State Tigerbelles and their storied success as world-class African-American female sprinters who collectively won 23 Olympic medals during the mid-twentieth century. Because of their supremacy in 100- and 200-meter races, a commonly held belief for many years was that African-American women shone primarily at short distances. (The same conclusion was reached about African-American men.)

Seven years before Rudolph won her Olympic gold medals in 1960, I ran the first of two childhood sprints. These runs were minor miracles. A year before my first sprint, I had gone to bed one night at home and awakened days later in a different place. A few minutes after I opened my eyes, I decided to get out of an unfamiliar narrow metal bed covered with a white sheet and a tan fleece blanket. A small table was to my left. When I looked toward my toes, I saw a black clipboard fastened to the foot of the bed. Voices from a hallway invaded the room. I sat up and swung my body onto the side of the bed. A short, stout woman with a frowning pecan-brown face rushed in as I tried to stand up. She caught me as I fell. What I learned later was that I had been in a coma for two weeks. The cause was life-threatening sepsis (blood poisoning). When I finally awakened, I was so weak that I could not walk. Regaining this ability required days of torturous attempts along hallways with cold-steel railings for people like me who might tumble. Finally, I mastered walking again, and I returned home. Mama blubbered as she drove me home from the hospital.

A year or so after my recovery, I had forgotten about this episode. My life went on as though I had never been ill. Around this time, I ran my childhood sprints. Their geneses were tied to an overwrought imagination with which I have been beleaguered or blessed all my life. My first sprint occurred after Joanne, one of my friends, and I strolled arm in arm one sunny summer morning from the one-room post office that served our community of Scotland, Maryland, where we had picked up mail for our families.

As we walked homeward, I turned around and saw a thick dark shape lumbering toward us. "A gorilla!" I shouted, taking off at a full-out run. Joanne looked behind us, and infected by my fear, she ran alongside me. Quickly, she passed me. Panicked, I extended my left arm and grabbed her shirt bottom just before it would have been moved beyond my reach. Summoning all my strength, I slowed her down.

"Let go of me," Joanne screamed, as she pushed my hands off her.

"That thing is not going to get me!"

"Stop!"

"Every time you try to leave me, I'm going to grab your shirt and pull you back."

"You're crazy."

"I'll stop only if you drag me along with you."

Grudgingly, she grasped my hand and tugged me along. We ran in tandem to Daley's General Store, where we rushed through the screen door to safety.

Peeking outside a few minutes later, we saw an old darkskinned African-American man shuffle by, his moth-bitten black felt hat askew on his untamed gray hair, his tattered black jacket held in place by its one remaining button and an enormous safety pin. Clutched in his fists were some white envelopes and a brown package.

Joanne glared at me. Grabbing my shoulders and shaking me roughly, she said, "You scaredy cat, you had us running from Mr. Hawkins."

After angrily slamming the screen door when she exited the store, she ran in the direction of her home, which could be reached only by traversing a narrow dirt path carved over decades by those who used it as a short cut from their houses to two destinations. One was a general store that catered to African Americans who sipped and slurped bottled root-beer and grape sodas and licked ice-cream cones as they lost money on one-armed bandits and listened to rhythm-and-blues tunes on the flaming-red jukebox. The other was St. Luke's United Methodist Church, where African-American Protestants worshipped on Sundays, enjoyed square dances on some Saturday evenings, and played baseball on Fridays during the summers.

Shortly after this sprint from danger, the second dash occurred. This time, though, I was alone. On this particular summer morning, I meandered to Joanne's house. Despite the Mr. Hawkins incident, we were still bosom buddies.

As I walked along the path through the woods, reddish-brown wasps huddled together, sipping sweet nectar from honeysuckle. Tempted to compete with them for the syrup, I resisted this impulse and reached instead toward emerald-green bushes with sweet-tart blackberries. After the tiny orbs burst in my mouth as I chewed them, dark syrupy liquid dripped from the corners of my mouth. I wiped the sweet-tangy juice off my face, staining my fingertips dark purple. After having my fill, I slowly continued on, daydreaming as was my way. A gray squirrel startled me, its patter the only sound other than fluttering birds' wings.

After I strolled along for a few more minutes, I heard a man's deep voice. Then I saw him. Clothed in black, the man called out in a deep voice, "Little girl, come over here." I screamed. I ran as fast as my skinny legs could carry me. When I burst through Joanne's front door, I was panting so heavily I could not talk. Her grandmother rushed toward me. "What's wrong with you, child?" she asked. I wheezed and grunted in response. When I was able to talk, haltingly, I said, "I saw a bogeyman." Joanne raised an eyebrow. "Sure it wasn't a gorilla?" she sharply inquired. Then she landed a knockout blow. "You're always seeing and hearing things nobody else does."

After resting and then gobbling a vanilla wafer and drinking a glass of water that her grandmother gave me, I pushed my fears aside temporarily and became engrossed in playing with Joanne's yellow-haired Bonnie-Braids doll. When the time came for me to leave, I refused to walk through the woods alone. Joanne, still doubting my story about the bogeyman, and her grandmother escorted me through the forest primeval.

NON-STOP HUMILIATION: NO MATTER THE GAME

Whump!!! It hit me squarely in the chest. Just skin and bones as a fourth grader, I had no cushion to soften the red rubber ball's impact. I toppled over, gasped, and struggled to breathe. Usually, the person behind the ball was Agnes, my elementary-school tormentor. She targeted me whenever she was on the opposing side of a dodge-ball game. As usual, I was the first person to be hit. I was not fleet enough of foot to outrun a ball thrown in my direction. For that reason, I was consistently the last person who was chosen for one of the sides.

Agnes seemed to dislike me from the first moment that I descended from the yellow school bus on my first day at the Jarboesville School, the public school for "colored" children in St. Mary's County, Maryland. Teasing me relentlessly, she called me Rapunzel so often that other students began to emulate her. When I complained about this treatment at home, Mama told me that my nemesis was jealous of my long wavy hair. Agnes's mother had attempted to straighten her daughter's hair with chemicals, and most of the girl's hair fell out permanently.

I left this world when I was 13 years old. For my parents, Baltimore meant greater employment opportunities just as such migrations had for millions of African Americans who moved en masse to urban locations from 1916 to 1970. For my sisters and me, this relocation meant, on one level, access to educational experiences that Saint Mary's County could not provide and, on another, more mundane, level, access to indoor plumbing, electricity, a Zenith television, and endless strips of crispy Goetze's bacon. In Saint Mary's County, outhouses, well water, kerosene lamps, and meatless meals had been our norm. While our lives improved in material ways when we migrated, we lost something, too. Our rootedness evaporated. No longer did we reside in a small place in which everyone knew everyone else's name and in which accountability was tied to these close connections.

In the short term, for me, this move meant no organized, or disorganized, games. The junior-high school that I attended, from which White students had fled years earlier, had no fitness program in place. My athletic experiences were limited to mad dashes after school to my family's rented row house, where I hid behind window screens adorned with crystal-clear azure lakes on which the whitest swans glided in the foreground and on which the whitest houses with the reddest roofs appeared in the background. In our neighborhood, a former side-show performer born without a lower body was the painter of such idyllic scenes.

I ran home every school day so that I could avoid students' settlements of their differences by tossing invectives at one another, by pulling tufts of dark hair out by the roots, and by throwing punches during full-out brawls. These frays usually began close to the school and moved, a swarm of bobbing heads atop brown bodies floating like herky-jerky marionettes eastward, into nearby trash-strewn neighborhoods in which African Americans overwhelmingly lived. Although I was never the prey of these hordes, I trembled in fear and horror whenever the bell announcing the end of school rang.

After I escaped from this barbaric school, I attended one of the first all-female public high schools in the nation. Approximately ten percent of the students were African Americans then. I felt like a bit of dark flotsam floating in white sea foam. Students here were required to participate in physical-education classes each semester. Whether inside the gym or outside on the playing fields, like the other girls, I wore a modest olive one-piece cotton gym suit with snaps down the middle, a matching cloth belt circling my waist, and bloomers fastened tightly around my thighs by elastic. White socks and white tennis shoes completed the outfit.

Regardless of the sport, I was consistently a poor performer. In softball, I could neither bat nor catch. On offense, I struck out every time. On defense, my assignment was always the outfield, where I just stood around. To my great relief, rarely did any of the girls hit the ball hard enough to come within ten feet of me. No doubt their failings in this regard were the reason that I was placed in this spot.

In basketball, I was equally inept. During my high-school years, girls' basketball teams had six players—three forwards and three guards. Forwards stayed in the front court and shot the ball. Guards stayed in the back court and tried to prevent the opposing team from scoring. Since every ball I tossed up was an air ball that began its descent almost immediately, I was always a guard. In the back court, I just stayed out of the way, the same approach I used when I was on the softball diamond.

While running events were not a regular part of the curriculum, we girls dashed occasionally across the jarring blond wooden floor of the gym, our shoes screeching like fingernails on a blackboard when we made sudden turns that occasionally twisted and sprained ankles. Gasping for air, I was consistently the last finisher. I never understood the reasons for these drills. What I did know was that physical-education classes were my most dreaded high-school experiences because they made me feel so bad about myself.

After high school, I attended one of the nation's premier historically Black colleges. My grades in the four physical-education classes required for graduation varied based on the type of athletic activity. I earned an A in folk and square dancing, not because I was an excellent dancer but because I was a good organizer. Grades were largely dependent on the quality of dances that groups of students performed. I herded the group of eight students to which I was assigned. I encouraged, wrangled, and nagged. Our professor required that each group master three dances, one of which we had to perform in front of the whole class. My group learned the hora, an Israeli circle dance that we practiced to "Hava Nagila"; the Virginia Reel, an English country-line dance that we practiced to "The Rattlin' Bog"; and the Tarantella, an Italian folk dance that we performed to "Funiculì, Funiculà." Our group chose the Tarantella for our performance to the class. Our brown faces bobbed from side to side as we bounced. Heads covered by scarlet scarves, we girls wore white peasant blouses and scarlet skirts dotted with white roses, and we banged tambourines on our hips and raised our arms in the air. Dressed in emerald-green shirts, the boys joined us girls, each boy dancing in a small circle with one of the girls. Visually, the group evoked the Italian flag. Our classmates raucously applauded our performance. A few of them stood up and whistled in appreciation. "That was great!" our professor exclaimed. Everyone in the group earned an A for the dance.

At the time, I did not think it odd that all of the dances that my group learned at a historically Black college had their geneses in European-folk tradition. This was the mid-1960s, a time when American-history textbooks included the Seventh Calvary, formed in 1866 and led by General George Armstrong Custer, but not the Buffalo Soldiers, the all-Black Tenth Cavalry, formed in the very same year, which fought in the Indian Wars.

My grades in physical-education classes steadily declined after I completed the dance course. I earned a B in golf. I fared this well because written-test performance determined most of the final grade. Students had no access to a golf course, and we had only a few putters for our use. Our skills at rolling a ball over a nine-foot green mat into a cut-out hole were evaluated and constituted the rest of the grade. In basketball, I earned a sympathy C. Mediocre at best, my college on-court performance was a repeat of my high-school experience. In elementary swimming, I received a D. As a child, I had almost drowned in the Chesapeake Bay during a church outing to Carr's Beach in Annapolis, Maryland. From the 1930s to the 1960s, it was one of the leading East-Coast beaches catering to African Americans. As a college student, I was still traumatized and was too terrified to learn anything in swimming class. This D grade could have obliterated my chances of graduating as class valedictorian. Fortunately, such was not my fate, for I had earned A's in all courses except golf, basketball, elementary swimming, and, inexplicably, introductory philosophy—the last course in which I earned a B, largely because I loathed the subject.

Braving Aerobics Classes

In the years between my college graduation and my 37th birthday, I engaged in virtually no fitness activities. To nudge me in this direction, David gave me a Spa-Lady membership as a birthday gift. Maybe I sounded out of breath when I walked. Maybe I complained too many times about rolls around my midsection.

The first time I slunk into this women-only fitness center, unpleasant memories of my past athletic failures overcame me. Also, discomfort about wearing body-revealing attire suffused me. When I removed my warm-up jacket and warm-up pants in the Spa-Lady locker room, I stared at my figure, primarily at my flattish chest and my pot belly, in a full-length mirror. I was clothed from neck to feet in a short-sleeved navy-blue leotard and matching tights. I wore a bra and full-cut panties underneath.

After 15 minutes of Jane Fondas (side-lying leg raises), abdominal crunches, and pelvic tilts, I was spent and drenched with perspiration. In two months, though, my athletic capacity grew so much that I became a high-impact aerobics maven, trading in my conservative attire for bike shorts with strategically placed rips revealing the tiniest bits of flesh, a matching low-cut bra, and an itty-bitty thong with matching leg warmers and headband. I kicked to the front, back, left, and right. I bounded. I swung from side to side like a pendulum. I jogged in place. Ear-splitting Patti LaBelle belted out "New Attitude." The Pointer Sisters revved the class up with "Pound, Pound, Pound." Sylvester transported us to new heights with "Do Ya Wanna Funk." My appetite for endorphins, serotonin, and dopamine (chemicals that decrease pain and increase feelings of pleasure) became so insatiable that I often attended back-to-back high-impact aerobics classes totaling two hours of almost non-stop bopping and hopping.

During these years, I was a professor and department chairperson at the Baltimore college where black particles fell like rain onto desks. Later, I held two deanships concurrently at the same institution. Somehow, I managed to leave my office twice weekly in time to attend aerobics classes. I even arranged my departures for vacations late enough in the day so that I could squeeze in grapevines, step touches, and v-steps.

After I retired, I planned to teach fitness classes. David was not surprised. He knew how much my view of myself as an athlete had changed since I began working out and how much my body had benefited. I lost body fat. My heart was stronger. My respiratory system improved. I wanted to help others to achieve similar benefits. However, when I told my friends, mostly professors, about my post-retirement aspiration, their uniform response was antipathy. Consistently, I had been associated with the life of the mind. My plans to change my focus to the life of the body seemed farfetched to them. They reminded me of a Greek chorus, a group of performers who register collective responses to the action in ancient plays. As one, my friends looked down their noses and inquired, "Why would you want to teach aerobics classes?"

Their comments puzzled me. To me, teaching facilitated discovery regardless of the setting and the subject. They ought to know how I felt. Just as I attempted to help my students understand the world of the Bennett sisters in Jane Austen's *Pride and Prejudice* (1813) and the universe of Pecola Breedlove in Toni Morrison's *The Bluest Eye* (1970), I aspired to foster growth in my future fitness students. At stake for my literature students was a deepened understanding of the limitations of women's worlds in early-nineteenth-century England and the impact of racism on an African-American girl in Ohio in 1941, respectively. At stake for my future fitness students was knowledge of ways to improve their physical health.

When I told David about the chorus's antipathy, he was not surprised. He said, "What do they know about fitness classes other than what they've seen on television or in movies?" Probably, he was right. If they had seen the 1985 movie *Perfect* in which Jamie Lee Curtis, dressed in a thong over a flesh-toned leotard suggestively thrust forward and rotated from side to side over and over again to up-tempo music with heavy bass lines, they might have thought that women in the field should not be taken seriously. They would not know that real-life exercise leaders rarely looked like Jamie Lee Curtis. They would not know that successful fitness instructors required knowledge of anatomy, choreography, and music. They would not know that, as a rule, fitness instructors led classes on a part-time basis because they enjoyed the sport. They certainly did not teach for the pittance they earned. Their full-time jobs varied. Some were nurses. Some were physical therapists. Others were public- and private-school teachers. During the years when I went to classes at least twice weekly, my favorite teacher was an accountant who taught a one-hour high-impact aerobics class two nights per week and was paid $25 for each class.

Ignoring the Greek chorus's head shaking, I trained for the future. Investing thousands of dollars in fitness-conference registration fees and in fitness-workshop fees, in hotel rooms, and in airline tickets, I traveled far and wide in the US so that I would be ready for my future profession.

I especially remember a trip to Cleveland, Ohio, where I pursued a group-fitness certification. Along with 20 or so aspiring instructors, all White women except me, I created and demonstrated sections of classes. Vividly, I remember leading an energetic warm-up to "It's Real" by James Ingram and being surprised a day later by the trainer's comment, "Some of your classmates wonder whether your routine yesterday would play in Peoria.'" "Huh?" During the vaudeville era, this midwestern city was a test market for show-business acts. The belief was that if performances in Peoria, Illinois, went well, the acts would be successful nationally. After the trainer's comment, I was confused. Thunderous applause had followed the warm-up. Were the music and the routine too urban or too Black or both? I never learned the answer. Despite this brief conversation, I departed the city as a certified group-fitness instructor.

I spent my time in Cleveland alone. David and Bryan remained behind in Maryland. However, they accompanied me on other fitness-training trips. When I learned how to teach step-aerobics classes in the City of Brotherly Love, they toured the Philadelphia Museum of Art and stared at the crack in the Liberty Bell. Bryan devoured gooey cheese steaks as David, a vegetarian, grimaced.

I mastered high-impact aerobics choreography in the Big Apple as David and Bryan visited the Empire State Building, the Statue of Liberty, and the World Trade Center. They stopped by Gray's Papaya, where Bryan scarfed down hotdogs slathered with the eatery's legendary red-onion sauce. Both father and son gulped down cups of the establishment's frosty orange-colored signature drink.

During these years, I earned and retained fitness-instructor certifications from the American Aerobics Association International, the American Council on Exercise, and the Exercise Safety Association. Even when years later I became a university chancellor, I earned continuing-education credits. Ironically, although I went to such lengths to ensure that I was ready to teach after retirement, I lacked the self-confidence to lead an actual class. Whenever someone encouraged me to teach from time to time, I hemmed and hawed, explaining that I lacked time to prepare.

Once, though, during the 1990s, I did lead a portion of a class. To my surprise, one evening my favorite aerobics instructor, the accountant, put me on the spot by inviting me to come to the front of the room to lead a routine. I did not have enough time to succumb to fear. Some of the women in the class started to applaud and yell out, "Come on, T. J. Get up there." I hurried to the front of the room and led the class for all of three minutes. The room erupted in loud clapping as I returned to my place in the first row, where I always stood because I was shorter than most of the women and could see the instructor better from this location. Also, positioning myself in the front was a habit from my school days when I, ever a nervous Nellie, chose my seat so that I could talk without seeing my classmates. If I saw them, my mind froze, and my hands shook as my words spilled illogically from my lips.

In settings other than my English-composition and literature classrooms, I dreaded public speaking—a major liability for an academic leader for whom panel presentations and speeches were responsibilities. But I hid my fear. Golden-oak lecterns and stark-white tablecloths prevented anyone from seeing my trembling hands and knocking knees. My audiences did not detect my dread. Often, I received kudos following presentations: "Insightful." "Great job!" "You speak so well!"

In 2014, after close to 20 years of preparation, I abandoned my long-held fantasy of leading fitness classes. The aerobics world had changed. Classes were canned. Prefab workouts such as Body Jam, Body Attack, Body Combat, and the like replaced instructor-designed classes. For participants, an advantage was that they knew what to expect regardless of who led the fitness session. For instructors, all they had to do was to memorize and regurgitate tried-and-true routines rather than tax their imaginations by creating their own classes. I told myself that I did not like this approach. In truth, I used this evolution as an excuse. I was still afraid.

Additionally, I convinced myself that I no longer wanted to pursue fitness indoors. Admittedly, some clubs offered outdoor boot-camp classes, but I found a way to disparage them as well. I told myself that while I enjoyed activities such as jumping jacks and lunges that could be done indoors or outdoors, I abhorred exercises such as slamming ropes and flipping tractor tires that were usually performed outdoors.

Because I looked toned after years of aerobics classes, people often assumed that I could run fast and long. However, aerobic training did not translate into running fitness. Dance elements common to such classes improved my aerobic capacity, core strength, coordination, and spatial awareness. These activities did not prepare me for running as I learned emphatically during my aerobics heyday when I competed in a two-mile parents' fun run at Bryan's school. I struggled to complete this seemingly never-ending distance in 28 minutes, gasping most of the way.

Grudging Move to a New Home

After David retired from the university in the Deep South, he accepted a position at a public high school in Randallstown, Maryland. Helping students to gain the mathematics skills necessary for success in a world that increasingly required technological proficiency was his mission.

Our house in Phillips Fields was 30 miles away, and he wanted to live close to the school, so we moved to a community that was about five miles away from his new workplace. Meanwhile, Bryan, who had been living with us, moved to a Baltimore-area apartment that he shared with his girlfriend.

Although our relocation dismayed me, I went along with the decision because of the proximity of miles and miles of streets on which I could run easily and safely. In our Phillips Fields neighborhood, I had access only to one and a half miles of asphalt within our development. I ran laps around and around this generally flat surface. On most days, a golden cocker spaniel named Cleo barked at me and chased me until I stopped and pretended that I was going to turn the tables and chase her. Then she retreated quickly into the safety of the arms of her female owner whose embarrassment was clear in her reddened face and in her words of apology.

If I did not run in Phillips Fields per se, two other nearby options were available, both of which were risky. I could venture onto the road bordering the community. It was the main corridor to and from Interstate 83 on which countless residents of the area's bedroom communities drove south during the week to office buildings in downtown Baltimore or to industrial parks located in suburban Baltimore or north to similar destinations in Harrisburg, Pennsylvania, and points in between. Dangerous for anyone on foot because it lacked shoulders, this road was also hazardous to human health because of noise pollution tied to honking horns and vrooming of vehicles on asphalt and because of air pollution tied to exhaust fumes and other vehicular emissions that caused me to cough, gasp, and choke.

The other option was a nearby nature preserve in which only a few people ran, walked, or biked. This was hardly an appropriate setting for a solitary female runner. David, however, cavalierly ran there without thought of possible perils. While he encountered no human adversaries, he was attacked by another menace. He contracted Lyme disease from a tick. Quickly, symptoms such as general fatigue, a rash resembling a target, and a throbbing headache appeared, and we rushed to a patient-care facility where, fortunately, a physician diagnosed him quickly. David began a three-week course of antibiotics and recovered fully.

While heavy traffic characterized our new neighborhood, once I walked or ran one-third of a mile and crossed Main Street in the historic section of Reisterstown, Maryland, extensive residential neighborhoods with wide streets and few cars and trucks were our new norm. During the morning and early afternoon, grandparents, parents, and babysitters pushed strollers containing yawning babies with wispy hair. Men, women, and children walked dogs or vice versa. Prospective customers dashed into nearby shops that purveyed coffee, collectibles, gently used clothing, and cast-off trikes and bikes. Clients strode into law offices, medical offices, tax-accounting firms, and beauty salons located in former family houses lining the streets.

For David and me, one of the neighborhood's main attractions was a high-school track. Once each week, we ran to this oval although rumor had it that it was a dangerous setting because drug dealers transacted business nearby. We never witnessed any suspicious characters. Usually, a purple-haired teenager running alone and white-haired and gray-haired walkers in ones, twos, and threes as well as students and teachers in physical-education classes were the only people other than us near or on the track. David was more disciplined than I was. Consistently, he completed the planned track workouts. I felt like a hamster on a wheel. I became bored, often announcing that I wanted to leave early but waiting for him, nonetheless.

Around this time, I went back and forth about joining a running group. David recommended that I seek advice from someone at Baltimore's oldest store specializing in running shoes, gear, and accoutrements. I needed new shoes, and he thought that a trip to purchase them was a perfect opportunity to learn about metropolitan-area running clubs. So off we went.

At the store, after I settled on a pair of jet-black shoes, I chatted with a salesperson about area running groups. She suggested the Pacemakers. Through the grapevine, I had already heard that these runners were super fast. I warned her that I was a running neophyte who was both old and slow. She replied, "The Pacemakers welcome new runners and experienced ones and everyone in between. Some of the runners are fast, but a lot aren't that fast." She encouraged me to try at least one run with the group. She gave me the email address of the group's coordinator.

Also, she told me about a women's training program that the running store sponsored and that she led once weekly during late spring and early summer. Ironically, the workouts occurred on a track on the very site of my high-school alma mater, which closed in the mid-1980s. The building had been transformed into a university's business offices.

During the once-weekly sessions, the group prepared for a 15K race (9.3 miles) in Druid Hill Park, a 745-acre park in northwest Baltimore. At least a third of the 30 or so women were good regional runners who often won age-group awards in local races. At least five of them had run in the Boston Marathon more than once or twice. A few neophyte runners were part of the group as well, but all I thought about were the fast women. I was out of my league, and I was instantly self-conscious about my inadequacies.

During the first session, in Baltimore's notoriously high summer humidity and heat, we ran once around the track, twice around the track, three times around the track, and four times around the track and sweated, sweated, sweated, and sweated as the coach called out our times as we passed her. I assumed that she was trying to learn what our baselines as runners were. Consistently, my times were among the slowest.

One of my favorite activities in later sessions was a run during which we formed groups of four or five women and ran in single file in our lanes on the track. After we started to run, the last person in the line sprinted to the front, making sure that she did not obstruct the path of runners in the adjacent lanes. Once that person was in place, the next person at the end of the line ran to the front. We repeated this process until the coach told us to stop. Maybe I liked the run because I was not timed individually.

During this period, David and Bryan occasionally commented on my new life as a runner. David effused, "I've never seen you exude such unbridled joy." Bryan joked, "The Jackie Joyner Kersee of the AARP set." I was befuddled by Bryan's reference to the African-American Olympic athlete. I never thought of her as a runner although an 800-meter race was one of the seven components of the heptathlon. Maybe she was one of the few African-American women athletes he knew by name.

Apprehension: Joining a Running Club

I was afraid I would not fit in.

Before my first Saturday run with the Pacemakers, I learned that the group, a loose confederation of running enthusiasts with no dues and no formal structure, numbered more than 200 runners. Usually, though, 50 to 80 people showed up for Saturday large-group runs. The weather and routes determined the number. Steamy conditions and snowy or icy conditions, predictably, led to a smaller group.

Most of the running routes, which changed from week to week, covered sections of Baltimore—such as Canton, Charles Village, Druid Hill Park, Federal Hill, Guilford, and The Johns Hopkins University campus. This running context translated into duels with speeding cars, numerous stops at traffic lights, an occasional desiccated rat glued to asphalt, broken soda and beer bottles and dented beverage cans, and uneven sidewalks like shifted tectonic plates that could easily trip runners and leave them sprawled in all directions on the concrete.

The composition of the group was consistent with national demographics summarized in *Running USA's State of the Sport 2010* report. This document includes responses to the *National Runner Survey* submitted by core runners—defined as active adults who enter races, purchase two to three pairs of running shoes annually, and run year round. In the US in 2009, the year I started running and the year I joined the Pacemakers, such runners were well educated. Approximately 79 percent held earned college degrees compared to 27 percent of the general population. Many Pacemakers met this standard. I never learned how many had earned which specific degrees, but I knew from conversations that many were white-collar professionals: attorneys, engineers, journalists, physicians, professors, and scientists. The participation of journalists was tied to the group's origin at a Baltimore newspaper during the late 1990s. Bob, the coordinator, had been a writer there when the group, four in number then, began as the Lunch Bunch. I fit in. I held an earned doctoral degree in English language and literature, and I had been a university professor and academic administrator during most of my career.

Gender demographics of the Pacemakers paralleled US trends. Nationally, women core runners outnumbered men. Such seemed to be the case with respect to the Pacemakers. But I never knew whether appearances were consistent with the facts.

Nationally, at the time, the mean age of women runners was 38.6. Women in the Pacemakers seemed to range in age from their twenties to a few in their 50s. I suspected that the mean age was close to the national average. As a woman in her mid-sixties when I joined the group, I was an outlier.

Nationally, on average, women core runners in 2009 had been participating in the sport for 11 years. Many of the women in the Pacemakers—even those who were latecomers to the sport—had been running for years and years. Some had been high-school and university runners. I had been running for approximately five months. Again, I was an outlier.

Racial demographics of the Pacemakers also mirrored national trends. Although Bob and two of the three other founders of the group were African Americans, more than 90 percent of the members of the group when I joined it were White. I did not remember meeting any Latina or Latino runners then. Only a few runners of Asian ethnicity ran with the group as far as I knew. I met only one person from the Middle East, a Palestinian woman who usually ran in a black hijab and in a long-sleeved solid-black tunic top and long black pants regardless of the weather. She must have roasted in this attire on hot days, but I assumed that her desire both to run and to honor her faith trumped any discomfort.

During my first Saturday-morning run with the Pacemakers, I met Wendy, a woman in her early forties whose renown on the comedy circuit was such that my son Bryan, whose avocation was stand-up comedy, knew who she was when I told him her surname (Adams). Initially, she and I ran at about the same slowish pace. Much more quickly and steadily than I, though, she ran up steep ascents such as Baltimore's TV Hill, the highest land point in the city and the transmitting site for four television stations and two radio stations. Later, I became faster and faster when we ran on flatter surfaces. As time went on, we stopped running together. Such breakups occur to running duos when one of the partners stops running in part or in full or when one of them develops race aspirations that the other person does not share. Also, as in life, sometimes partnerships change when one of the runners simply prefers the company of others.

Around the time when my partnership with Wendy ended, I started running with a subset of women in the Pacemakers who opted out of the group's 5:30 a.m. speed-work sessions on a Baltimore prep-school track. I lived 20 miles from the school and had to get up at 4:00 a.m. to dress and drive there in time to run with the Pacemakers. Never an early bird, I loathed rising at this ungodly hour. The women's group met at 6:00 a.m. at the only water fountain at Druid Hill Park for a four-mile easy run or for speed work. I got to sleep in until 4:30 a.m.—a whole half hour. Hooray!

For a few years, on Mondays and Wednesdays, we ran together. Speed workouts occurred infrequently, and when they were included, they were random and scattered with no overall plan tied to specific paces and distances. Hardly a true replacement for the Pacemakers' speed sessions at 5:30 a.m. No problem for me. I was simply happy to run with other people during the week.

Although I had the longest drive, I was usually the first or second person to arrive. By 5:55 a.m., everyone had normally appeared. Including me, we were seven in number and were a study in ethnic diversity and a study in commonality in our love of running: five women of European descent—Angela, Dawna, Eileen, Julie, and Rita; one woman of Asian descent—Takiko; and one of African descent—me. Three of the women were attorneys. One was a newspaper journalist. One was a brain scientist. One was a professor as I had been.

On these mornings, after sniffing David as was my primal way, I dragged myself from his just-warm enough but not-too-warm body and his light snoring. After dressing, I stumbled into the garage and pushed the button that raised the door, squeezed past David's car, and sprinted to my car, which was parked on the street. I drove slowly to the community gatehouse. Impatiently, I counted every second as, at a glacial pace, the black steel gate wobbled like an off-balance oldster toward my vehicle. Narrowly, the gate avoided smacking my car's grill. I never understood the thinking behind the installation of a gate that opened toward cars and trucks.

About 25 minutes later, I rolled into a parking space near the fountain. The other women and I warmed up by running clockwise around the 1.4-mile paved bike path encircling the lake, actually a reservoir. As we ran along, we barely glanced at the marble-walled Moorish Tower, standing more than 30 feet tall. Overlooking swaths of Baltimore, it dated from 1870 and had been designed, along with whimsical Chinese-style pagodas that dotted the Park, by the municipal architect at the time. We passed by a six-foot marble statue celebrating Christopher Columbus, hardly a surprising sight given that Baltimore had attracted thousands of Italian immigrants dating back to the late 1800s. We ran near another statue, approximately 40 feet tall from its base to the tip of a drawn sword held by William Wallace, the honoree. After my first sighting of this imposing statue, I was curious about how this fourteenth-century Scottish hero who led his countrymen against England in a fight for his country's independence came to be honored in this setting. I learned that people of Scottish descent had long held high-level positions in Baltimore and that the statue, a replica of one on a Scottish hill, had been donated during the late 19th century by successful Baltimore banker and Scottish immigrant William Wallace Spence, who claimed to be one of the hero's descendants. Hmm. I was born in Scotland, Maryland. A connection of sorts.

After we ran past the Tower, the Columbus statue, and the Wallace statue, we crossed over a road on which we dodged cars even in the dark morning hours. When a member of our band was late, she ran counterclockwise to meet us before we left the lake area and, we hoped, before we began our gradual ascent to the Mansion House, the former residence of the colonel who sold the Park's lands to the city of Baltimore. After we descended, we often ran to the abandoned reptile house—an overgrown shell of a yellow-brick structure that housed alligators, terrapins, and diverse other reptiles and amphibians from the late 1940s to 2004 when financial exigency forced the building's closing. Occasionally, we ran instead to the brightly colored Baltimore Model Safety City, where school children learned how to be safe pedestrians by walking through a miniaturized model of downtown Baltimore. Once, we ran to Pool No. 2, built in 1921 to serve African-American water enthusiasts. The pool closed when Baltimore public pools were desegregated in 1956. What we saw during our run was a former pool that had been filled in with soil on which green grass grew in abundance. I had not known until then about its existence.

Frequently, I needed to tinkle after running one or two miles. I did not know then that this frequency was abnormal. Although a few porta-potties were scattered here and there in the park, the foul odors emanating from them and concern about what or who might greet me after I opened the door prevented me from entering. My resistance was reinforced when one day a member of the group stopped to relieve herself inside a dull-green portable restroom and a city vehicle that resembled a dump truck pulled up, placed a fork-lift device under the porta-potty, and began to raise it into the air while she was inside. Fortunately, one of us—I do not remember who—saw what was happening and yelled, "Stop! Stop! There's someone inside" and jumped up and down while making continuous X's with her arms until the driver noticed her. The likelihood of a recurrence was slim, but watching this scenario unfold reinforced my belief that I should opt for outdoor spaces whenever I had urinary needs.

When I began with the all-women crew, I was the slowest runner although I had gone through the women's-training program and had run several races without embarrassing myself. To my dismay, during one of these early days, a group of seven or eight Pacemakers running together in Druid Hill Park came upon me as I trailed our little group. Snidely, one of the women pointed toward my running buddies and asked, "Are you with them?" I responded, "Yes. Why do you ask?" She countered, "You're so far behind I thought you were alone." I could feel my face warming. I turned slightly away from her so she could not see my discomfort. In hindsight, I understood that my lack of familiarity with the setting, my greater age, and my inability to run fast until I completed a few miles were the reasons I trailed the group. As time went on, keeping up became less and less of an issue, especially after I began to arrive early and warm up a bit before anyone else came to the fountain.

For me, one of the greatest virtues of our small group was that the women encouraged me. Especially I remember how they always waited for me during my first ascents with them to the Mansion House, clapping their hands and shouting "Way to go" when I crossed a brick rectangle that marked the top. I felt as though I had won an Olympic competition. After six weeks, I climbed upward quickly. I could have beaten others to the top, but I hung back. I was not in a race, so I did not care about being out front.

We had several running rules. One was that nothing that was said during the run was repeated. Following this rule was easy for me, for I generally ignored the chatting. Another rule was that we never left anyone behind. Although few deadly crimes occurred there, the Park was sketchy. From time to time, people were victims of robberies or of thefts from their cars. Occasionally, homeless people pushing shopping carts or toting their belongings on their backs sat on benches inside pagodas from dawn to late at night. Too often, deranged people roamed and raved. Sometimes if they latched onto someone, these Park visitors followed the unfortunate person around spewing warnings about the Rapture or some other apocalypse. Once one of these people, a gray-haired matronly woman, gyrated in my direction and babbled and gesticulated until I managed to elude her. On one of the strangest mornings in the Park, a woman rapidly descended from the Mansion House and cautioned as we ran upward, "Stay in the middle. They're near the edges." We saw no one as we moved along. We never discovered who "they" were.

Usually, by the time our runs ended and we returned to the fountain, the Park was in full swing. Young swaggering African-American men with rippling muscles pumped free weights they had brought from home and exercised on city-provided rowing machines on sunny days. Often, one or two of them shadow boxed and skipped rope. In another time and place, they might have been hunters with spears in their hands and might have been attired in tribal garb, perhaps bright red to frighten away lions. Instead, in this setting, they were American-Dream-chasing want-to-be professional prizefighters wearing black boxing gloves to protect their hands and gray polyester workout shorts to cover their sculpted thighs. African-American women in twos or threes chatted as they leisurely circumnavigated the lake over and over again. Solo African-American women power walked while they chatted on their smart phones. Gaggles of African-American graybeards bantered about politics as they sat on, rather than used, stationary fitness equipment. Young White couples from nearby Charles Village pushed strollers in which babies with rosy cheeks nestled. Red-faced students from the Homewood campus of The Johns Hopkins University, which bordered the Park, sprinted. On many mornings, a thin middle-aged woman with a side-view mirror mounted on her violet helmet circled the lake like a spinning top on her top-of-the-line road bike time and time again.

While the Park became a familiar setting, I rarely knew much about the neighborhoods in which the large Pacemakers group ran on Saturdays. The routes varied from week to week. I did not have the luxury of arriving late and catching up with the group as I did on Mondays and Wednesdays when I ran with the women's group. I was on my own, and in deep trouble, if I reached the starting point after the group departed. On the few occasions when I was late and ran alone, I misinterpreted the turn-by-turn route sheets that Bob left on the windshield of his car for latecomers and became lost and had to rely on the kindness of strangers to find my way.

I was so anxious about arriving on time that I sleepily asked David the same question each Saturday. After rubbing my fists over my eyes, I inquired, "What time is it?" The clock was on his side of the bed, and it was positioned so I could not see it. His silver hair and wiry runner's body blocked my view. He probably thought he was trapped in *Groundhog Day*, a movie about a weatherman who becomes ensnared in a temporal loop and lives the same day over and over again.

After questioning David about the time, I usually asked him, "Do you know what the temperature is supposed to be this morning?" Sometimes he knew because he had checked the night before. Usually, though, he did not know specifics but had a general idea, so he would respond perfunctorily by saying something like "Supposed to be in the forties and overcast, I think." Almost always, I replied, "I'll check weather.com as soon as I get up." He probably wondered why I bothered him with the question when I could easily find the answer myself, but he never complained.

After each long Saturday run, the Pacemakers congregated in a restaurant or coffee shop at the same location where they began and crammed into booths and at tables where they inhaled breakfasts of steel-cut oatmeal, fluffy pancakes, crisp bacon, cheese-infused grits, and other morning-menu yummies. Sometimes so many people stayed after the runs to eat and talk that no spaces were available for other customers.

Occasionally, instead of coming together for runs and ending at restaurants or coffee shops, we met and ended at the home of one of the runners. On one Saturday morning in early fall 2010, about 25 of us Pacemakers sat on a runner's white porch that wrapped around the rear of a red-brick colonial in a planned neighborhood in Baltimore. Slowly, we munched on homemade blueberry strata and homemade bagels that our host, an attorney, and his wife prepared for the group's post-run brunch.

A woman runner teased me about my crop top and my matching running skirt. "Where are your lime-green shoes?" she asked, giggling. Smiles appeared on the faces of a few runners within hearing range. I laughed and responded, "I'm wearing yellow and gray today. Those shoes don't match this outfit. Also, my green shoes are lightweight-performance shoes. I wear them only when I'm running fewer than five miles. Today my run was an LSD." To the non-runner, perhaps my use of this term might have suggested that I had "tripped" on a mood-altering substance, but the acronym was commonly used by runners to refer to long slow distances (endurance runs at a low or moderate pace for an extended number of miles).

The woman's remarks about my clothing and shoes were tied to my persona as a "stunner" (a blend of two words, "stylish" and "runner"). *Runner's World* used this label for runners who dressed fashionably. Counter to runners who proudly sported frayed five-year-old shorts, usually black, and snagged t-shirts with race names printed on the front and sponsors listed on the back, I consistently wore color-coordinated outfits. As my suits and pumps had masked my discomfort and self-doubts in professional settings, so my running clothing and shoes hid similar feelings in this context. When I ran alone or when I ran only with David, I thought that I paid little attention to my appearance. I was disabused of this notion when a biker passed me one summer morning when I was running solo. He observed, "You're the best-dressed runner out here."

As a few other Pacemakers and I lounged on the yellow-and-green plaid cushioned sofa on the porch, a 20-something woman sporting an auburn ponytail, bounced in. She said that she was new to the group and that she was late joining us for the post-run socializing because she had covered 20 miles. Most of the rest of us had run no more than 14 or 15 miles.

She told us about her preparation for the Richmond (Virginia) marathon. She twinkled as she rambled on about the high percentage of finishers—more than 20 percent, she claimed—who ran this race fast enough to qualify for the Boston Marathon. I stood closest to her, chatting with other runners. After the others walked away, the newcomer turned to me and said, "I overheard some of the runners congratulating you on the hardware you've won recently." Smiling like someone who's pulled a fast one, I said, "I've done all right. When you're old, the odds that you'll win age-group awards improve. Not as much competition."

She asked, "How old are you?"

"Mid-sixties," I responded.

She gasped. "Gee," she said, "I would have guessed that you were 45."

Secretly, I relished telling people how old I was just so I could lap up their amazement when they learned the truth.

I said, "If you want to endear yourself to me, next time you should guess 35."

Both of us giggled. Then she inquired, "Do you ever think about how great you could've been as a runner if you'd started sooner?"

"No," I responded flatly.

TOO MUCH OF A GOOD THING: RACES, RACES, RACES

During my first year as a runner, I threw myself into racing. After I competed in the Maryland Half Marathon, I ran in eight 5Ks (3.1 miles); one 10K (6.2 miles); one 15K (9.3 miles); and one additional half marathon (13.1 miles). My participation in 5Ks was tied primarily to their proliferation rather than to my thinking that I had any special ability at this distance. Most weekends during the spring, summer, and early fall, consistent with national trends, 5K races abounded in the Baltimore-metropolitan area. My 12 races in a single year exceeded the average for a "core runner," whose average in 2009, according to the *National Runner Survey*, was seven races.

A month after the Maryland Half Marathon, I ran in my very first 5K, a women-only race in downtown Baltimore that occurred on June 28, 2009. The race was challenging for two reasons. I did not know then that I should warm up by running before a 5K. I placed myself too far in the back, behind happily chatting walkers spread across the breadth of the course. The race was a social event for them, and they seemed to have planned to ambulate in this way during the entire 3.1 miles. When I saw an opening, I jumped onto a sidewalk. I stubbed my toe. I very nearly fell to my knees. As soon as I passed the walking women, I leaped down onto the asphalt street. I sprinted to make up time. Running strongly for the rest of the 5K, I finished fifth of 24 women in the 60-64 age group. My time was 30:19. My pace was 9:45. I had hoped that I would run faster.

Two weeks later, things began to look up when I ran in the Pikesville 5K, which occurred in a suburb about 15 miles west of Baltimore. At this point, I knew the importance of a short pre-race warm-up that raised my temperature, prompted blood flow to the muscles I would use, helped me to achieve a breathing steady state, and relaxed me. I warmed up by running slowly for approximately one mile after which I walked to the start line and positioned myself near the front of the pack.

This 5K course was more challenging than the downtown race, but my time was 45 seconds faster. I placed second in my age group and won my first running honor, a 6" x 9" free-standing clear acrylic award. I was pleased with my performance until a woman, a running coach I had met by chance when I was preparing for the Maryland Half Marathon, took me aside. She had come in first in the 50-54 women's group. In response to my second-place age-group award, instead of praising me, she blurted, "You need to run harder." I was taken aback.

After being chastised, I trotted over to the results table to see whether I could train hard enough to win first place next year if the same cast of characters ran then. The woman who won first prize in my age group was four years younger than I, and she had completed the race in four fewer minutes. I moaned aloud, "It'll be a miracle if I run that much faster in just a year." Of course, the possibility of her not running the following year was always there. Even though I was new to competitive running, I already knew that, for every race, the likelihood of winning an award was a function of who showed up. I also knew that, to increase the likelihood that they might win awards, some runners studied past years' results to scope out the likely competition. If faster participants usually ran in some races, award-hungry runners might avoid these events and select less competitive races instead. In later days, I became guilty, too, of choosing races that past results suggested that I would most likely win an age-group award.

The following year, I learned, even if the woman who came in first in my age group toed the line again in the Pikesville 5K, her performance would not affect me. By then, I would be in the 65-

69 group. This woman would still be in the 60-64 group. I would have to deal with other runners.

Three weeks after this second-place finish, I ran in a hilly 5K that was sponsored by a Jewish women's organization. With dead legs because I had squatted and lunged too much during a fitness class the day before the race, I stopped halfway for a few seconds, resumed running, summoned a reservoir of energy that I did not know that I possessed, and sped across the finish line. Although I ran 25 seconds slower than I had in the Pikesville 5K, I came in first in the 60-64 women's group. This outcome reinforced once more what I already knew—that winning race awards depended on who competed.

On the heels of this 5K, I ran in two more races in quick succession. The first of these was a 10K sponsored by a Catholic men's group committed to community service. The race occurred in a hilly section of nearby Howard County, an area in which I had never run. Alone, I drove the route a few weeks before the race. My focus was on learning about the hills. On race day, I realized that my surveillance had been faulty. I had miscounted the number of hills. I conserved energy so that I could run up the fifth, and I thought the last hill, only to discover several minutes later that there was a sixth hill. I was so pooped when I ascended the final hill that I threw away my water bottle to get rid of the negligible weight. Gasping, I crossed the finish line—at last.

I finished first of two women in my age group. My finishing time was 1:00:43, and my 10K pace was 9:46, around the same pace of my 5Ks. David thought that my consistent pacing regardless of the distance meant that, once I reached a certain speed, I could hold that pace for a fairly long time. I was built for endurance, he proclaimed.

In a burst of patriotism, a week after the 10K, I competed in Baltimore's Run to Remember 5K, a mid-week race on

September 11, to commemorate victims and first responders associated with the 2001 terrorist attacks. Icy rain, unusual for this time of year, pelted the runners and took its toll on my music player, which died about five minutes after the start. I learned then that I could run without tunes, a surprising discovery. Instead, I moved to the rhythm of the unrelenting downpour and to the sound of my feet slapping the wet pavement. I finished third in my age group, which was made up of four women. My time was 30:43. My pace was 9:53, not that bad given the conditions.

Two days later, I participated in the Falls Road 15K. I decided that I would reach the finish line before a good runner I knew who was at least 15 years younger than I. I did not know then or later why I zeroed in on her. Competitive to the core, I fed off her during the race. Every time that she came within a few feet of me, I surged. I would die on the course, I vowed, before I let her pass me. She never knew that I used her presence to push myself to run faster and faster. My gun time was 1:29:25. The race sponsors provided no timing chips to runners, so net time was not captured. My pace was 9:35. In my age group, I came in first of two runners. The woman with whom I competed crossed the finish line after I came in. This was my third, and longest, race over an eight-day stretch. It was also my fastest pace in the three races. David appeared to be right about my being able to hold my speed at longer distances.

A month later, I ran in the Baltimore Half Marathon. The somewhat hilly half-marathon course began downtown in Baltimore's Inner Harbor and continued through sections of East Baltimore and then north through The Johns Hopkins University campus before heading south and back downtown. At the time, I had not run in these neighborhoods often enough with the Pacemakers to develop route memory, and I had not practiced on the half-marathon course on my own. Had I practiced the route several times, I would have most likely registered a faster time than I did. This lesson was one that I did not forget when I prepared for future races.

Also, I learned a second lesson on race day. I made the mistake of wearing new socks. Rain fell briefly at the start and dampened my socks. During the first half of the race, my feet felt as they normally did. Then the bottoms of my feet began to sting during the second half. Severe pain increased with every step I took. Reduced to walking, I finally crossed the finish line. Immediately, I sat on a curb and removed my shoes and socks. Blisters filled with clear liquid dotted my toes and soles. I should have tested the socks during training runs and under differing conditions prior to racing in them.

In spite of this challenge, my net time of 2:18:32 was almost ten minutes faster than had been my time in the Maryland Half Marathon five months earlier. My pace in the Baltimore Half Marathon was 10:34. I finished seventh of 47 women aged 65 to 69. I should have taken solace in finishing in the top 15 percent of a much more competitive and much larger field than had run in my first half marathon when I was fourth of 12 runners in my age group. However, I was crushed and embarrassed. I had told friends and relatives that I was running. I had anticipated that I would finish much higher up.

During the next five weeks, I ran in four 5Ks. My slowing times during the first three of these four reflected my increasing fatigue. The first of the four I ran eight days after the Baltimore Half Marathon. My net time was 31:35, and my pace was 10:10. I was second of six women. A week later, I ran a 5K in which my net time was 31:51, and my pace was 10:15. I was second of ten women in my age group. During the third 5K, my eleventh race of the year, I was so fatigued that I could barely run. Halfway through the race, I wondered whether exhaustion would force me to walk the final mile and a half. My net time was 32:29, and I was second of three women in my age group. I had become a bridesmaid.

To redeem myself after this slow race, I competed once more that year, chasing a better time. I was shocked that the race, a Thanksgiving Day Turkey Trot with 1,234 participants, used gun time to determine order of finish. As soon as this realization came to me, I crept to the front and began the race with the fast people to ensure that I lost not a single millisecond. Runners who started farther back had little or no chance of winning awards; they would lose too much time before they crossed the start line. The finish of the race was unlike anything that I had experienced in the past. When each runner crossed the finish line, volunteers tore off the perforated bottom section of the bibs and gave each slip to a man who placed it on a giant safety pin. Several people sat at a table and typed away as each runner crossed the finish line. I wondered how accurate the times would be, given the hordes of people who crossed the finish line close together. My time was 31:01—almost a minute and a half faster than my most recent 5K net time on a course of similar difficulty. My pace was 9:58. My improved time was a function of a three-week rest and my running the course twice before the actual race. I was third of eight women in my age group and received a 20-pound turkey and a certificate in honor of my achievement. I promptly gave the turkey to a family of four standing just beyond the finish line. One of my sisters was hosting Thanksgiving dinner later that day, and I had no room in my freezer to store the turkey for a future meal.

DETERMINATION: A POST-EXHAUSTION RETURN TO RUNNING

Exhausted physically and mentally, I went on a racing hiatus for six months—from November 27, 2009, to May 1, 2010. I considered abandonment of the sport. Since running staved off my demons by elevating my mood, I stuck with it, learning during my first winter as a runner that this season brought a new set of challenges—icy footing that could lead to falls and to breathing difficulties. During this period, I was diagnosed with exercise-induced asthma and received an Albuterol prescription.

When I began to race again, winter and its challenges had long gone. Heat was a major problem on May 2, 2010, when I ran in the Frederick Half Marathon in western Maryland. By the final half-mile of the race, I was torn about how I should respond to the conditions. I was so conflicted that I conjured up two versions of a miniaturized woman runner, identical in most ways, riding on my shoulders. On my left side, she held a red pitchfork and urged me to slow down. A sly smile appeared. Entrancingly, she muttered, "Take a walking break. Then pretend you've been running the whole time when you see the finish line. Sprint so the race photographer snaps you finishing at break-neck speed." On the right side, the miniaturized woman runner was dressed entirely in green and had a firm, determined look plastered on her face. Steadily, she pounded rapidly on a tiny drum the cadence at which I should be running. I heeded the figure on my right shoulder. Continuously, I ran, although slower than her drumbeat.

Four hours before I crossed the finish mat, David and I had parked in a grass-covered field near the race start. Dawn had not yet begun to light the day, so we walked cautiously to the area where the race was to begin. I wore low-cut socks, and cooling dew splashed on my ankles. The humidity caused my running top to stick to my skin. The temperature was in the 70s already, and the humidity was over 90 percent. The day before, runners had been warned that high heat and high humidity warranted adjustments to their expectations. This would not be a race that yielded personal records.

Why had I registered for this half marathon? Of course, I knew the answer. Bob had recommended it. He said that the course was flat. When I shared his description with one of the women in the Pacemakers, she chuckled. "Why did you believe him?" she asked. Later I learned that the other Pacemakers were in on the joke. They knew that Bob described steep hills as inclines and torturous routes as easy strolls. I forgave him when he surprised another Pacemaker and me by popping up on the course and running with us. While running alongside them during the first few miles, I made two mistakes. First, I ran too fast because I was trying to keep up with them. Second, because Bob drank Powerade, the drink provided by the race organizers, I sipped a few ounces, too. I had never put lips to this beverage before I made this bad decision. Full-throttle nausea ensued quickly. At the end of the half marathon, I made another poor nutritional move. A volunteer near the finish line offered me half of an orange. Hungry, I gobbled it down although I had never, prior to this time, eaten citrus fruit at the end of a race. Five minutes later, masticated orange pulp spewed from my mouth and my nose. Violent spasms of my torso quickly followed. David, standing near the finish line, reached out to steady me.

I finished third in my age group that torrid day. My time was 2:15:24. To my shock, I ran three minutes faster than I had completed the Baltimore Half Marathon. Running was like life, often unpredictable.

Three weeks later, I improved my half-marathon time again. The course of the second Maryland Half Marathon was much hillier than the inaugural version. When I confessed my trepidation about the route during a conversation with a local running-store owner, he suggested that I conserve energy by walking as fast as I could up the steepest hill and then regaining as much time as possible on the downhill and the remainder of the race. I followed his advice. I ran down that hill as though werewolves were chasing me. Finishing in 2:13:21, I was third in my age group, running two minutes faster than I had in the Frederick Half Marathon. I was jazzed to have won another age-group award. Better than fourth place at the end of the inaugural Maryland Half Marathon. And on a tougher course.

A Would-Be Predator in a Car

From time to time, I ran solo on the streets of Baltimore or Reisterstown. I gave little thought to my vulnerability. I was usually in places bubbling with people, so I trotted along without a care when men in cars slowed near me or seemed to be following me.

Thus, I was quite comfortable one Saturday morning when I ended up running solo after a woman in the Pacemakers began a 12-mile route with me but stopped after three miles because of pain associated with a chronic knee injury. I sped off alone, running quickly, at least for me, about three more miles south to downtown Baltimore, where I encountered Bob, who told me to run south for another block and then make a U-turn and return to the start of the route. A half-hour later and nearly three miles closer to the end of the run, I passed huge brick colonials in which the wealthiest Baltimoreans lived. I spaced out until I forced myself to pay close attention to where my feet landed. Small piles of fresh dog feces dotted these ritzy streets. As I jumped from clear spot to clear spot, I felt as though I were playing a variation of hopscotch.

After moving onto streets with less poop, I ran strongly for another mile or so fantasizing about myself as an older Fatuma Roba—the first African woman to win, in 1996, an Olympic Marathon. Then I began to fade. I had brought along only one energy gel, and I had consumed it at the start of the run. I needed at least one more to sustain myself until I reached the café where the run had begun.

As I slowly made my way, sometimes I hopped onto concrete sidewalks. When the sidewalks ended, asphalt streets covered with wet newspaper ads, denuded pine cones, and smashed soda cans became my sole running surface. I faced zooming vehicles speckled with caked-on grime. When I could not dodge the oncoming traffic any longer, I came to a dead stop, positioned my back against parked vehicles, and flattened myself, hoping that I would not lose the tips of my toes, which were pointed toward the cars and trucks whose heat I could feel on my face as they sped by.

A mile or so from the end of the run, a small bright blue "toon car" with so many splotches that it looked like an acne-scarred Celtic warrior slowed down. Out of the corner of my left eye, I saw the auto, but I kept on moving. The driver appeared to be a 50-something White male with stubble on his cheeks and chin. His hair was probably, I deduced, blonde once but was now mostly white. So large that he appeared to have been stuffed into the vehicle, he smiled broadly and mouthed something. I was listening to music. Then the man's thin lips moved again. A thought popped into my head. He looked like the humongous father in *The Incredibles* movie who drove an itty-bitty car. I had watched this 2004 Walt Disney animated comedy about a family of superheroes at least five times on television and often guffawed loudly as I watched the formerly muscular Mr. Incredible, relegated from superhero to a paunchy white-collar employee and suburban dad, force himself into his too-small automobile.

Why was he stopping on this street? If he needed directions, he was in trouble. I had no clue about the streets in this neighborhood. Still smiling, he asked, "Do you need a ride?" I was offended. Did I look so tired that strangers were offering me rides? "No, thanks," I said, staring coldly at him. I ran harder and faster just to show him that I still had some juice left.

Fifteen minutes later as I sat in the café with other Pacemakers and drank coffee with too much half and half and just enough artificial sweetener from a yellow packet and munched on a cheese-broccoli-artichoke soufflé with far too many calories, I told Bob about the encounter with the man. He looked at me carefully.

"Yeah, we would never have seen T. J. again if she'd accepted that ride," he said to Pacemakers within earshot.

I retorted, "As if I'd hop into a stranger's car."

Only then did I understand that I might have been in peril. The driver might have gotten out of his car and forced me inside. Broad daylight was not necessarily a shield. Neither was the presence of other cars. The more cars and the more people, the less likely was the probability of intervention. In social-psychology theory, this phenomenon is termed bystander apathy or the bystander effect. People inside these vehicles would have probably thought that someone else would come to my aid and would have continued along their way.

Invoking Mama's Inner Toughness (My First Marathon)

On Saturdays, I began to run primarily with Eileen from the Druid Hill Park women's group. A mentor, she slowed me down during long runs by asking me questions that I felt compelled to answer. Initially, I did not realize that her forcing me to talk was a deliberate effort to oblige me to run at a conversational pace, which was at least a minute slower per mile than my aspirational marathon pace. When I was going to be late for a Saturday-morning run, I telephoned her, and she waited for me, the two of us tackling the streets of Baltimore in darkness—sometimes encountering women and men on their way home from nights of working or partying. One memorable morning, a woman with black eyeliner smeared like a ragged path down her nose, sparkly gold and green three-inch nails, and a broad smile revealing a gold canine tooth exclaimed, "Ladies, you looking good." It followed as the night the day that when I ran my first marathon, Eileen influenced my decision. One of her favorite courses was the Steamtown Marathon, a race that began in Forest City, Pennsylvania, and ended in Scranton, Pennsylvania. The marathon boasted a net downhill profile and was consistently included in lists of top Boston-Marathon qualifiers.

When I sought a running plan, David recommended that I read Hal Higdon's *Marathon*. Higdon's 18-week novice plan became my gospel as I trained. I believed so fervently in his system that I jokingly referred to him as Saint Hal. For the beginning marathoner, his book prescribed four days of running weekly. Novice runners completed no speed work. Endurance was the focus. As prescribed, I ran a half marathon eight weeks into the schedule and ran 20 miles once, during the 15th week, and tapered (reduced my mileage) during the final three weeks of training.

Clank. Clank. Clunk. Shudder. The noisy elevator caused me to wince. The shaft was next to my "superior" seventh-floor room in the Scranton Hilton, the city's finest accommodations. Sprawled face down across a rust and tan comforter and buried beneath beige linen pillow squares and oblongs, I tried in vain to ignore the sounds. I needed to sleep. The marathon began in a little more than 36 hours.

At 7:00 a.m. on the following day, Saturday, October 9, I telephoned the front desk. Fortunately, a female customer-service person answered. I believed that a man would have been more likely to be dismissive. Even with her, I knew I had to sound like a White woman. Black people often accused me of sounding White, so conveying this impression was easy. All I had to do was to speak as I normally did. Also, I knew that I could not let her see me before she agreed to change the room. Denying a request from an African American would be easier for her than saying "No" to a White person. Once I explained my problem, she responded not as I expected initially. In spite of our common gender, she subjected me to the party line, "We're full and can't offer you another room." I retorted, "All of your guests haven't checked in yet. Give one of them this noisy room. I've got to sleep tonight. I have my first marathon tomorrow." She hemmed and hawed but then agreed to help me. "I'm too swamped now, but I'll find you another room. We'll move you this morning." I waited for an hour. When she did not call, I telephoned again. She told me that I could come down to pick up the key to my new room. After sleeping about eight hours that night, I awoke at 5:00 a.m. on Sunday, October 10, and walked to one of the nearby yellow school buses that would transport hundreds of runners to the high school where the race began.

I was calm as I jogged to the start line. Uppermost in my mind was the weather. The fastest marathons are run when temperatures are in the 40s. As the temperature increases, times decline, by five minutes when temperatures are in the 50s and by almost 20 minutes when the mercury rises to the 70s. Winds matter as well. Fighting the wind, especially headwinds that retard forward movement, burns valuable energy.

The temperature was around 32 degrees, and I shivered a little. The temperature would rise as I ran toward the finish, so I was grateful for the cold. Winds were negligible. The sky was bright and clear. So glorious! Clothed in a black throwaway jacket over a water vest, I began my maiden marathon. To ensure that I did not fall prey to overexcitement and a too-fast start, I ran at the rear of the group. I exhorted myself, "Warm up during the first five or six miles. Run more quickly but not too quickly as the miles roll by."

During the first mile, I began to perspire so profusely that I tugged my jacket awkwardly off and tossed it aside. As was the custom during many races, volunteers would walk along the route later and collect jackets, sweaters, hats, and gloves that would be donated to charities throughout the region. Clad now only in an emerald-green sports bra and a black running skirt, I ran comfortably. Succumbing to superstition, I later chose to wear this bra in every race in which I ran thereafter.

In two hours and eight minutes, I crossed the halfway mark and struggled to contain my energy. Approximately 20 minutes later, after running another two miles or so on asphalt, I clopped over a small wooden bridge spanning the rushing, transparent Lackawanna River. Soft, soothing wood chips greeted me on the other side. Relishing the tree-lined rails-to-trails portion of the race, I sank into this gentler surface—blessed relief for my tiring feet. Awed by the crimson and gold fall foliage on each side, I acknowledged my good fortune to be able to run so far at my age. I purred out loud, "I've found my distance—the marathon." I hummed along for a few more miles, forcing myself to slow down when my watch showed that I had run my last mile at 8:50 pace. I had wanted to pace myself at about 9:30 per mile.

Suddenly woozy, I staggered like a broken-down Palooka. I began to walk. Hoping to restore my equilibrium, I ripped open one of the gels I carried in my water vest's front pocket. After slurping this dark-brown syrup, I chased it down with tepid water. David's pre-race advice popped into my head. "Perpetual forward motion. Never stop completely. Even when you're fueling, move in the direction of the finish line." I tottered toward Scranton.

At the moment when I was sure that I would topple over, a lurking Lackawanna County mini-bus, black with a red roof, circled like a scarlet-pated turkey vulture patiently awaiting fresh road kill. The "SAG wag" is not going to get me, I vowed. Only if I'm unconscious. At that moment, I thought about how David teased me about my pre-race references to this vehicle. He claimed that I made up the term. But I had not. Initially, a SAG, an acronym for a support-and-gear wagon, was a vehicle carrying cyclists' gear. The term migrated over time into road racers' argot and referred to a vehicle used to transport runners who are ill or too slow to finish races by designated cut-off times.

Motivated by an admixture of fear of failure and tough mindedness, I kept going, alternating between walking and running. I chanted, "Hurricane Hazel" as I inhaled Mama's spirit—her strength as she, in 1954, carried both her one-year-old daughter and her two-year-old daughter in her arms and marched her four older daughters, aged four to 11 years old, on foot to shelter on higher ground. I could still hear Mama's threatening us with thrashings if we disobeyed her as we trudged on, holding hands to form a human chain through swirling water, tree-bending winds, and bruising rain. We were walking from the low-lying southern-Maryland farm on the water's edge where we had been living with the couple who 32 years earlier had stolen her from her fourteen-year-old birth mother. My parents were estranged yet another time, so Daddy was not there to help Mama. I was nine years old then, and throughout my entire life, the trauma of this trek haunted me. Constantly as I moved toward the marathon's terminus, I reminded myself, "Remember that you're Mary Bryan's girl." When I waned, I chanted "Mama, Mama, Mama" over and over again.

This mantra strengthened me until I reached the final few miles of the race. What Eileen had not mentioned when she described the race was that the course rose near the end. Immediately before I saw the incline, I thought I was home free, especially when a man grinned at me and proclaimed, "It's all downhill to the finish." Cruel to the core!

Walking more than I was running at this point, finally, I saw the finish line and summoned enough energy to dash across it. My chip time was 4:42:07. My pace was 10:46. I was fourth of six women in my age group.

When I crossed the finish line, I joined a group with relatively few members. According to *MarathonGuide.com*, in 2010, 503,000 runners in the US finished marathons. Women made up a little over 41 percent of this group. Women in my age group (65-69) made up a little more than .5 percent of women finishers. This percentage translated into 1,056 runners. Running reports did not collect racial or ethnic information about runners, but I was fairly certain that a tiny fraction of the female marathoners who were 65 to 69 years old were African American.

Covered with so much salt on my face, my legs, and my arms that I gasped in shock when I glimpsed my reflection in a mirror in the Scranton Hilton's lobby, I staggered back to my room, where I lay inert on the bed for at least an hour. I forced myself to step gingerly into the shower. I rotated the water-temperature knob to the most forceful and hottest settings. Initially, my back burned in spots where my water vest had rubbed patches of skin off. After a few minutes, though, I was oblivious to the stinging sensations. I remained rooted to the shower floor for at least 30 minutes.

Although I did not win an age-group award, I garnered something that was far more valuable. I ran fast enough to qualify for the 2011 Boston Marathon—with close to three minutes to spare.

Encounters of the Surreal Kind: Training for the 2011 Boston Marathon

Twice as I trained for the 2011 Boston Marathon, I was transported from the real to the surreal.

One frozen morning six months before the race, as I ran in Reisterstown, a dented black compact car chugged so close to me that I could have reached out and touched it. I felt isolated as I ran alone. Ashes dripped from a red-tipped cigarette trapped between the middle and index fingers of the dirty-blond-haired driver's left hand. I wondered how his fingernails could be so dirt encrusted at the beginning of the day. Maybe he worked at night and was on his way home. For a few seconds, his startled pale-blue eyes seemed to be as focused on me as my brown ones were on him. What he saw was a small not-so-young African-American woman running alone in 20-degree weather through a politically conservative neighborhood of red-brick ranchers. Their postage-stamp yards were dotted with red, white, and blue signs supporting the Republican candidate for Governor of Maryland in the upcoming general election. Slowly, the car chugged away, becoming a smaller and smaller black dot and then disappearing over the crest of a distant hill.

I focused on moving through piles of brownish-gray maple leaves with long stems intact. The blustery wind blew them left and right. A few leaves gently hit my face. Had I been in one of the Baltimore neighborhoods where the Pacemakers usually ran, I might have thought that the errant leaves were long-dead rats brittled by time's passage and flattened by automobile tires. After an hour, I tired, but I had to climb one more hill. If I reached the top, I told myself that Mama would be waiting there. I pushed myself, chanting, "Do it. Do it. Do it."

There she was when I reached the crest of the final hill. Although the air was frigid, Mama wore only a white terry-cloth robe and a thin purple nightgown. Taller by four inches than she was, I easily glimpsed, when she turned her head for no reason, the tiny thinning spot that had been on her crown for years. Furtively, I stole a look at her back. No fluffy white wings sprang forth.

She stared at my head covering, with its black background, large red roses, and white skulls and cross bones.

Sticking her right index finger into the material, she asked, "What's this thing?"

"It's a Buff."

"A what?"

"A Buff. I can wear it as a bandana or a scarf."

Although I sounded knowledgeable, in fact, I had only recently learned what a Buff was. I had gone to an outdoor-attire and outdoor-equipment store to find a balaclava to cover my neck and mouth on cold mornings. I had never shopped in the store before this visit. Almost immediately after I entered, I felt as though a red-haired salesperson in her mid-30s was watching my every move. As an African-American woman, I had long been aware of the phenomenon called "shopping while Black." A few years before my visit to this store, a January 2009 *ABC News/Washington Post* poll revealed that 54 percent of Black respondents believed that they were treated poorly by retailers. For Whites, the figure was 15 percent. A Black person might be followed around a store or closely watched by clerks or guards because of the suspicion that shoplifting might occur, or a Black person might be denied access to specific merchandise. (Even Oprah Winfrey reported having been denied the opportunity to examine a handbag in a Switzerland leather-goods store in 2013. The clerk allegedly told her, "It's too expensive.")

I had hoped to avoid such treatment by styling my hair conservatively and by wearing a modest fitness outfit. Perhaps, I might be accorded the same courtesies that White clients usually were. Additionally, I engaged the salesperson in conversation. I could invoke my impeccable command of standard English as I had during my stay at the Scranton Hilton.

As we talked about my needs, she made a case for my selecting a Buff by asserting authoritatively, "The contestants on *Survivor* wear them." So what? Why would I care what they wore? "I'll buy just one," I said. After I wore my Buff a few times, I decided that I liked it. Later, I bought several more—from a different store.

Mama interrupted my reflections. She stared at my head.

"Did you comb your hair this morning?"

"No, Mama. I'm wearing the Buff so I don't have to do anything to my hair before I go out in public."

She shook her head in bewilderment.

Then Mama plunged her right hand into the depths of her robe pocket and brought forth an enormous black rubber shampoo comb with at least a half-inch space between each set of stout teeth.

"Turn around," she softly growled.

I squirmed as I stood with my back to her.

"Girl, stand up straight."

She pulled the Buff down so that it encircled my neck. She spread her fingers over the back of my head, and then with her right index finger against my scalp, she drew a line with the comb and separated each half of my hair. Gently, she smoothed down wandering strands and pulled the Buff up over my neatened hair.

On the heels of this surreal running episode, I tumbled down another rabbit hole. During this period, David and I rarely ran together. He loved silent solo trail runs. However, because four inches of snow had fallen overnight, he did not want to drive his sports car, which fishtailed as soon as someone mentioned the word "snow," to a state park where he often ran on technical trails (challenging routes with steep climbs and descents, rugged rocks, treacherous roots, knee-deep water, and slippery mud). That day I had my own concerns about driving into Baltimore to meet the Pacemakers. I feared becoming trapped in a mound of snow on some random street, a real concern given that the city had an abominable snow-removal history.

David planned to run ten miles that day. I wanted to cover 13 miles. Close enough! We decided to drive to Druid Hill Park in my car and tackle our miles together. We agreed to run slowly during the first two miles, but I sped up. He complained, "If we don't tone it down, I'm not going to be able to finish even eight miles." I forced myself to run at 10:45 pace, which felt like a crawl. As we moved along, a squirrel startled us. Nonchalantly, it strutted directly across our path. David exclaimed, "That squirrel behaved as though we weren't here. It didn't even hurry." I responded, "That thing must think it owns this park. Somebody ought to run over it."

I bent over to retie a shoelace that was coming undone. David ran ahead of me. When I looked up, he was about a tenth of a mile in front of me. Curious, I looked around to see where the squirrel had gone.

Suddenly, it rushed toward me. Copping an over-the-top attitude, the little rodent swaggered toward me. It squeaked,

"Hey, bitch! I heard what you said about me. Who're you calling a 'thing'? I took my time because this is my turf. Here I do whatever I want." Without taking a breath, it continued, "Anytime I want, I can get my gang to come here and swarm you. You'll never get out of this here park alive."

I was flabbergasted. I began to mumble. Appearing to seize upon my confusion, the squirrel moved its head from side to side like a cobra, raised the palm of its paw in front of my face, and then squeaked, "Talk to the hand because the ears ain't listening." I closed my eyes for about five seconds. The squirrel was still there when I opened them. Then I blinked rapidly. I told myself, "You've lost your mind." Instead of pinching myself to ensure that I was not trapped in a nightmare, I repeatedly bopped my forehead with the heel of my right hand.

Quickly, I ran in David's direction. I did not want to look behind myself, but I could not resist. The squirrel still stood in the same spot. Staring straight at me, it raised the long middle digit on its right paw.

When I caught up with David, he asked, "What were you doing back there?" Too quickly, I responded, "Just communing with nature." As I continued my training for the 2011 Boston Marathon, the squirrel's dressing me down became a distant memory.

For the next few months, I followed my schedule of running with the Druid Hill Park women's group on Mondays and Wednesdays, with the large Pacemakers group on Saturdays, and with myself only twice a week in Reisterstown.

In accordance with Saint Hal's novice marathon plan, I ran in a half marathon midway. This race was the 2011 Baltimore and Annapolis (B and A) Trail Half Marathon—my fifth half marathon in two years of running. Exhilarated for some forgotten reason and feeling fortunate because the weather at the start was ideal, with a temperature in the low 40s and light rain, I ran my fastest half marathon ever on this paved rail trail in Maryland's Anne Arundel County. At one point, I looked down at my GPS watch and saw that I was running at 7:15 pace. I could not sustain this speed, so I forced myself to dial back the pace. Even after taking this step, I finished in 2:01:04—26 minutes faster than my first half marathon, 17 minutes faster than my second, 14 minutes faster than my third, and 12 minutes faster than my fourth. My pace was 9:16. Nothing like positive emotions and superb weather.

Halcyon Days: My Third, Fourth, and Fifth Marathons

My halcyon days as a marathoner began six months after the 2011 Boston Marathon. My new running partner was the main reason. Bill Rodgers (Boston-Marathon winner and New-York-City-Marathon winner) had Amby Burfoot (Boston-Marathon winner and Olympic marathoner) as his training partner. Shalane Flanagan (Olympian and World-Championships runner) had Kara Goucher (Olympian and World-Championships runner) as hers. I had Margaret.

I met her one Saturday during a Pacemakers' run. I was running alone. That day Eileen had other plans and was unable to join the group. I already knew who Margaret was. Often, she was the subject of other runners' conversations. The foremost topic was her streak, which had been the focus of a newspaper article years before I met her. A member of the United States Running Streak Association, she was touted for running at least one mile each day on the roads or on a track or on a treadmill for years. Nationally, she was one of a small percentage of streaking women. In addition to this achievement, rumor had it that Margaret once held a women's age-group US record for 800 meters. I never knew whether the gossip was based in truth. Later, when we ran together, I did not inquire.

I could not fathom why she invited me to join her. She was much faster than I. She said we complemented one another. "You can run forever, and I can run fast. Let's help one another." Although we lived far from one another, each week we ran together three times. On Tuesdays, I drove 70 miles round trip to her house, and on Thursdays, she drove the same distance to my house. On Saturdays, we met at the Pacemakers' launching spot and ran together. Usually, she was out front, but she always came back to wrangle me. She was the Jedi master teaching me about facing oncoming vehicular traffic, about running on the right side on trails and other places without cars and trucks, and about using New-Skin liquid bandage for small cuts and scrapes.

As time went on, Margaret and I wore similar running outfits on some Saturdays. If I saw a top or a skirt that I liked, I bought two items—one for each of us. She followed suit. One Saturday, a male Pacemaker, so muscular and so magnificently dark hued that he evoked a sculpture of an African warrior, did a double take when he saw the two of us rushing to the start of the run. He asked, "Am I seeing double?" He needed Mr. Magoo's glasses. No one ever thought that Margaret and I looked alike. At 5'6," she was three inches taller than I. More conscientious than I about what she ate, she boasted a toned, taut torso. Muscular, especially her legs, she left David awestruck when he glanced at her lower body. He claimed that he had rarely seen female quadriceps and hamstrings as massive and as sculpted as hers. Regularly, she was mistaken for a professional athlete during our runs. No one mistook me for such. The difference between us was so striking that a woman in the Pacemakers observed, "You two resemble Mutt and Jeff." I was not amused by her comparison of us to these two mismatched comic-strip characters, one tall and the other short. But I had to admit that we probably were as dissimilar when we ran together as two people could be. Margaret had a long loping stride while I shuffled. To keep up when we ran together, I took far more steps than she. My average cadence was usually around 190 steps per minute, my GPS watch indicated, while Margaret's was close to 180, she told me. She exhibited just the slightest bounce in her stride. When I ran, my feet were so low to the ground that David once said, "There isn't enough space between your shoes and the ground for a single sheet of paper to pass."

Over time, when I registered for races, Margaret helped me by practicing, when possible, with me on the actual routes so I could increase the likelihood that I would run well. By learning about courses and running on them, we followed in the steps of legendary elite runners. Olympic 10,000-meter gold medalist and World Championships 10,000-meter gold medalist Haile Gebrasalassie of Ethiopia, often considered the greatest distance runner of all time, famously studied racing routes. Olympic marathon gold medalist and silver medalist Frank Shorter of the US knew that reconnoitering was key to deciding when to surge, when to hold back, and when to go for broke.

Calculatingly, I avoided uphill races, for such courses usually translated into slower finish times. I was a downhill runner by predilection, probably because, unlike many runners, I did not suffer trashed quadriceps (the severe stressing of these muscles because of deceleration forces and impact absorption) because of my relatively light weight, shuffling stride that reduced the likelihood of heavy pounding, and quick turnover that lightened my footfall. Additionally, through practice, I gained speed with minimal effort, using gravity rather than strength to pull me forward and down as much as possible during descents.

Although Margaret and I ran hundreds of miles as a training duo, we ran only one race together. I preferred to compete alone. Racing with a partner meant allowing someone else to enter my zone. I violated my rule of solo racing once, though, before I ran my single race with Margaret. I ran with Jenny, a Pacemaker woman in her early 40s who often invoked me as her running role model. I luxuriated in her admiration. Perhaps, ego drove me to run with Jenny on October 9, 2011, when I tackled the Steamtown Marathon a second time. For 20 miles, she hummed and sang along to Bon Jovi hits such as "Living on a Prayer" and "You Give Love a Bad Name" as well as a bevy of other songs popularized by rock bands. After a few miles, I was able to ignore her off-key vocalizing. However, I could not block out the sound of her feet pounding the earth so heavily that I wondered whether I was running next to a herd of elephants. At mile 21, I no longer heard her footfalls. She surged and left me in her dust.

I could not keep up with Jenny at this point because, at the start, I ran faster than was my norm and used up energy that I usually reserved for the final quarter of the marathon. She usually rocketed from the jump. Automatically, I reverted to my longtime role of teacher. As we covered the miles, I warned her about the course's inclusion of a school track around mile 13, about the bridge spanning the Lackawanna River, and about the ascent near Scranton, where the race ended. When I reached the finish line, she sat on the grass sipping a sports drink. Immediately after I saw her, I rushed to check my time. I finished the race in 4:23:51, a little over 18 minutes faster than my finish time a year earlier in this same marathon. My pace was 10:04. I finished second of seven women in my age group.

By the time I returned to Maryland, Margaret had surmised what had happened during the race. She chided me, "I know how you run. You always begin slowly. You sacrificed yourself by running fast at the beginning of the race. And then she left you, didn't she?" I was not upset about Jenny's darting away. I would have left me too if the situation had been reversed.

A month later, I trotted alongside Margaret in the Richmond Marathon, the only race we ever ran together. David was apprehensive about my running so soon after the Steamtown Marathon. I risked injury and slower times, he said. I responded, "I'm already trained, so what's the big deal?"

I drove alone to the host city on Friday evening. Margaret and her husband arrived on Saturday afternoon. I happened to run into them at the packet-pickup location as I was about to hop onto a bus that transported runners over much of the race course. The preview did not lure her. I next saw her the following morning near the start of the race.

Margaret considered the marathon a training run. I did not. The term was not in my vocabulary. From the start of the Richmond Marathon, I ran with the single objective of improving my marathon finishing time. When we passed a Pacemaker woman who was struggling during the second half of the race, Margaret asked me, "Should we 'pull' her?" To "pull" this runner, we would have to slow down to motivate her with encouraging words and run at a pace that the woman could handle. Although this runner was one of my favorite Pacemakers, I responded coolly, "You can do whatever you want. I'm running as fast as I can."

I usually kept moving after 26.2 miles to avoid cramping and dizziness. Conventional wisdom was that such motion keeps oxygenated blood circulating through the body and ensures equilibrium. As soon as I crossed the finish line, however, I stopped to talk with Bob, who was standing nearby. Margaret had dashed ahead of me during the final mile. She always smelled the barn whenever we neared the end of a run. Crossing the finish line close to a minute before I did, she stood there and applauded as I came in.

Suddenly, a gray-haired woman with narrowed eyes and a brisk walk rushed toward me with a wheel chair. She ordered, "Sit here." Protesting, I told her, "I'm fine." She replied, "You're not fine. I'm a nurse. I know when someone is about to faint." She wheeled me into an arctic tent and helped me onto a table where a male paramedic inserted a needle into my arm. Margaret and her husband followed. Teeth chattering, I told the paramedic, "I'm freezing. I need a blanket." Next to me were other tables on which other athletes lay. After this, my first-ever post-race intravenous rehydration, I recovered quickly. With Margaret and her husband, I walked slowly to a restaurant where the Pacemakers who competed in the race and their family members planned to meet for lunch. We arrived in time to order along with everyone else.

After the Richmond Marathon, when I attempted to check my race time, my name did not appear in the participants' list. When I returned home, I telephoned the Richmond Marathon organizers and inquired about my missing data. The person to whom I spoke asked me if I had run with someone else. When I provided Margaret's bib number, he told me that someone would check photographs and videos of her along the route to find evidence of my running with her. The race organizers found abundant proof of both of us running side by side. Whew! I received credit for the marathon. My finishing time was 4:21:48, and my pace was 9:59. I finished first of ten women in my age group.

Later, I realized what had happened. On the morning of the race, I pinned my bib to my running skirt before I rode to the race start with some of the Pacemakers. When I sat down in the car, my bib, which had the timing chip embedded, folded across my hips. Unknowingly, I broke the built-in antenna. This was the first race in which I had run that used such a bib, and I had not known that I could destroy the timing mechanism. In all my earlier races with chip timing, I had worn a small plastic tag on my shoe that tracked my start, my progress on the course, and my finish.

Five months later, on April 22, 2012, I competed in the Glass City (Toledo, Ohio) Marathon. I traveled with Margaret, who ran in the half marathon while I ran in the full. After picking up our race packets and checking into the hotel, she and I began course reconnaissance. In waning daylight, she drove through sections of the route that were accessible by car. We knew that this trip would not reveal information about nuances that a true run would. It was better than nothing, however.

The next morning the race began on the University of Toledo campus. Weather conditions were ideal. The temperature was around 40 degrees, and the sky was clear. I was a little rattled by a notice that I read in the instructions in the race packet. Runners were cautioned about their responsibility to navigate the course. I wondered whether runners had gotten lost in the past and hence this caveat was included.

Impulsively, during the second mile, I fell in with a 10:15 pace group. I became a bit concerned when one of the people in the group said loudly that the pacer was running too fast. I remained with the group, nonetheless. A blonde woman who appeared to be in her 50s ran near me. I stared at her. She introduced herself. I forgot her name five seconds later. She hailed from England.

As she and I ran together, a scene for which the nighttime-course review did not prepare me unfolded. Suddenly, black, white, tan, and brown monsters with long necks, webbed feet, and flat bills appeared as we ran briefly through Toledo's Wildwood Preserve Metropark. Canada geese evoked terror in me no matter where I encountered them. In the broad scheme of perils, they were second only to bears as animal dangers to runners. When a group of geese honked and squawked and then waddled in my direction, I feared for my life and limbs. These creatures were approximately half my 5'3" height and probably weighed around 20 to 25 pounds each. Their wingspans were wider than I was tall.

The British woman appeared unflustered by the menacing creatures. To her, I probably looked unfazed as well. We ran in tandem until we reached the 21st mile. Then I tired and could no longer keep up. About a mile after we parted ways, the lace on my right shoe became untied. I was shocked. This unfastening was a first for me during a race. I had double knotted the lace, but I had not tucked my laces inside my shoes as an additional precaution. Quickly, my body became so cold that, when I stopped to tie my shoe, my hands became stiff and numb. As I stood on the course sobbing like an abandoned toddler, a wiry male runner saw my dilemma and rushed over to tie my shoe. "I might as well stop to help you," he said. "I'm having a bad day."

A mile later, I realized that I was out of glycogen. I had no gels left. Trying imperfectly to imitate race walkers I had seen in televised Olympic competitions, I synchronized my arms and my hip motion and moved as rapidly as I could for a few minutes, and then I ran for as long as I could. Desperately, I alternated between pseudo race walking and running. I knew that I would finish the marathon, but I wanted to finish first in my age group. The woman who had won the 65-69 division a year earlier was on the course. I knew not where.

Around mile 24, Margaret appeared. We had agreed that she would meet me on the marathon course around this point and "run me in" (accompany me until I was a few feet from the finish line). Smiling, she announced, "I came in second in the 55-59 female age group." I was so tired and cold that I barely listened to her. Margaret tried every trick in her repertoire to encourage me to move quickly. "Run to that lamppost," she urged. "You can make it to the next corner," she encouraged. "You're too good a runner to give up now," she cajoled. I convulsed in laughter when she appealed to my vanity. "You don't want a course photographer to take a picture of you walking." Mixed in her urging was a confession. "You should be glad I keep my word. The last thing I wanted to do after sitting in the warm car was to come back out here to run with you."

Finally, we reached the University of Toledo. Although I heard the race announcer calling names of runners as they crossed the finish line, I did not know where I should go. No signs directing runners were visible. No course marshals were around. Confused and frustrated, I felt like weeping again. All that I could think about was the warning in the race materials that runners were responsible for knowing the course. I moaned, "Margaret, I don't know what to do." She comforted me. "I know how to get to the line. Just follow me. I'll peel off as soon as I know you see the finish." Seconds later, in a surprising burst of energy, I triumphantly dashed across the mat and heard my name announced.

After a volunteer draped a finisher's medal around my neck, I jogged, energized, to the results table, where I learned that I was first in my age group; I had finished ahead of three other women. I expected an acrylic or metal award in recognition of this achievement, but, to my surprise, I received royal-blue running sleeves with a Glass City Marathon logo embossed on them as well as a large powder-blue athletic bag. Apoplexy! I wanted something to add to my carefully arranged shelves of racing awards.

The Glass City Marathon was my fifth 26.2 race and the fifth time that I qualified for the Boston Marathon. My finishing time was 4:22:39. My pace was 10:01.

For this brief halcyon span, consistency characterized my marathon times—4:23:51; 4:21:48; and 4:22:39, respectively. I hoped this pattern would continue.

A Grateful Return to Racing: My Sixth Marathon

In mid-May 2012, a few weeks after the Glass City Marathon, I stopped in my tracks yelping. After running ten miles during a weekend Pacemakers' run, I could barely walk. My right foot felt as though it had broken in half. Hobbling back to my car, I stretched this foot every few blocks. Every time I halted, a Pacemaker seemed to materialize from out of thin air to ask an identically worded question, "Are you all right?"

What I learned a week later after a visit to a podiatrist was that I suffered from plantar fasciitis. The thick connective tissue that supports the arch was ruptured. He prescribed physical therapy to strengthen and stretch the plantar fascia, lower-leg muscles, and Achilles tendon. Also, he required that I wear a night splint, a boot that gently stretched the foot and held the ankle at a 90-degree angle, while I was in bed. The premise was that the plantar fascia and the Achilles tendon would maintain elongation while I was in a horizontal position and that my condition would be resolved more readily than otherwise. For me, wearing the device was so uncomfortable that I removed it every night after about five minutes in bed. When I confessed my inability to follow instructions with respect to the splint, my podiatrist told me to put it on when I was sitting so that stretching occurred during the day at least.

This injury meant that I could not train for the 2013 Boston Marathon for which I had qualified. While I had planned to run in the Boston Marathon just once, I changed my mind on a whim and had registered a second time. David could not accompany me. He had classes to teach at the high school and did not want to miss them. My youngest sister, who was then chancellor of a community college, agreed to go with me. She would meet me near the finish line, in almost the same spot where David had waited for me two years earlier. I would need to lean on her as I stumbled back to the hotel where I had reserved two separate rooms because I did not want to share a space with her. I needed alone time.

Since I was not prepared, I did not go. I had already paid the registration fee for the marathon, purchased a nonrefundable airline ticket, and made a deposit on two hotel rooms. I had to "eat" the cost of the registration fee. The Boston Athletic Association did not give refunds or allow deferral to a future race. I could have used the airline ticket for another trip, but I did not redeem it. I lost the deposit on the rooms.

My sisters claimed that my injury was divine intervention. To anyone who listened, all five of them rhapsodized about Mama's ability to affect our lives from beyond the grave. Perhaps they were right. My past marathon times suggested that I would be approaching the finish line around the time that homemade pressure-cooker bombs left by the Tsarnaev brothers, two self-radicalized men of Chechen descent, exploded. These improvised explosive devices caused the deaths of three spectators and injuries to 264 people, including 16 who lost limbs. If my sister had waited for me at the agreed-upon spot, she would have been in harm's way.

David speculated that my running three marathons in seven months, from October 2011 through April 2012, was my undoing. And he might have been right. Conventional wisdom was that runners should limit themselves to no more than two marathons annually. A single marathon was the ideal. Running the marathon distance too often increased the likelihood of injury and slower times, largely because the body and mind became worn down. That I was cruising toward injury never occurred to me.

I was sidelined for fourteen months. During this timeout, I went to a fitness club four days per week. In addition to attending classes such as Body Pump and Aqua Sculpt, I haunted the cycling studio and became a spinning maven. At the back of the peloton, I climbed, climbed, climbed up imaginary hills. In the middle of the pack, I sprinted on imaginary flat ground. I glistened, glistened, and glistened with sweat, not ladylike perspiration, after each session. Thirsting for other ways to burn energy, I attempted, in individual lessons, to swim twice weekly. Sinking like a boulder, I spent most of my time sitting in the five-foot-deep section languishing in blue chlorine and marveling at swimmers with abilities I might never possess.

On May 25, 2014, resurrection as a runner was mine. I ran in a 10K and finished first in my division. According to the race results, my finishing time was 1:00:36 with a pace of 9:46 per mile, but according to my GPS watch, my time was 59:52 with a pace of 9:38 per mile. When I whined to David about the discrepancy in the times and paces, he explained, "You ran farther than the race distance. If you divide your time by a slightly longer distance, your watch will show a faster pace." He added, "Unless you hit all the tangents perfectly in a race—and that would be almost impossible, you're bound to run farther, and your pace won't agree with the timing company's numbers."

David explained further, "When courses are set and verified for distance, corners are cut as closely as possible. If a road has a bunch of curves, for example, the measurer doesn't follow along the edges of the curves. Instead, he or she goes as straight as possible, an act that might mean running from a curve on one side of a road to another curve on the other side of the street."

He continued, "Remember when your GPS watch registered 26.45 miles at the end of the 2011 Boston Marathon? You said that you ran back and forth to the sides of the roads so that you could slap hands with children. You added distance in that way, and you probably did a lot of weaving throughout the race."

I did not think about tangents or the accuracy of my GPS watch a few months later when David and I ran a half marathon together on Maryland's Eastern Shore. All I could think about as we started to run was that, for this race, my reconnaissance backfired. When I registered us, I reviewed the route on the race's website, where the course was presented from the vantage point of a camera attached to a bike. After studying the route, David and I drove one weekend to a hotel near the race's start. After spending a night, we arose early the next morning and practiced the course.

A month or so later, on race morning, we showed up at the start, a deserted former outlet mall. No one was there. We were positive that we had the correct date for the race. We drove around this ghost mall for several minutes before we saw a woman walking a dog. David stopped the car. I rolled down the passenger-side window and asked her, "Where does the race begin?" She frowned. "What race?" she asked. In unison, David and I said the name of the race. She responded, "You're in the wrong place. The race started here last year, but this year it begins at the high school." David and I stared at one another. Then I realized that I had printed last year's race information. We picked up our bibs and schwag bag the day before at the high school. I was so sure I knew everything I needed to know that I had asked no questions.

David accelerated the car so forcefully that it squealed in surprise. We sped toward the high school. Quickly, he parked the car, and we sprinted to the timing table where an emaciated-looking man with a droopy white mustache sat. He leaned toward us as we explained that we had gone to the wrong place. Calm, he grinned slightly. He said, "The race started 45 minutes ago." He added, "We're using chip timing, so you can go ahead and run." Joyously, I exclaimed, "Thank you. Thank you. You're so nice to let us race." Drily, he said, "You'd better get going."

Anxious, I began to run too quickly. David muttered, "Slow down. You're not going to make up 45 minutes during the first mile."

Despite the curve that I had thrown us, we ran well. When we practiced for the race, we had moved in single file, alternating the lead at the beginning of each mile. We implemented this plan on race day. He led the first mile and all the other odd-numbered miles while I led the even-numbered miles. I embraced this division of responsibilities because he led seven miles compared to my six.

Quickly after we began, we realized that we had practiced only part of the course and that the route did not unfold as we had practiced. The abandoned outlet mall, where we thought we would begin the race, was close to midway. A business park that we trotted through during our practice run and an oyster-shell path that fascinated us because it was so different from our usual running surfaces were not part of the race at all. Instead, we ran through a community of misty-green, cotton-candy pink, baby-blue, and other cheerfully hued faux-Victorian houses that we had never seen before.

At the beginning of the twelfth mile, I was too tired to take my turn as the leader. When David realized what was happening, he said, "See you at the finish line." I could not believe my eyes as I stared at his shoe soles as he abandoned me. His finish time was 2:09:49, and mine was 2:10:41. He was first in his age group, and I was first in my age group. There was one other man in his group. I was the only woman in my group.

Despite our winning age-group awards, I was livid. "You left me," I reproached him. Gleefully, he responded, "I 'spoused' you."

"What does that mean?"

"I finished before my spouse crossed the line."

He laughed. I scowled.

The organization that benefited from the race was a group of Christian churches that raised funds for food, shelter, and clothing for the region's neediest residents. After calming down, I soaked in post-race good vibes. I asked David, "Do you think we were allowed to run because of the special kind of people who undertake good works?" He replied, "Could be. Certainly, everybody we've met here has been super nice."

Two months later, I ran in the Potomac River Marathon, my first marathon attempt in two and a half years. The setting—the Chesapeake and Ohio (C and O) Canal Towpath—enthralled me. In operation from 1831 to 1924, the Towpath was the surface on which mules had walked as they pulled barges loaded with coal, produce, furniture, and other items along the canal adjacent to the Potomac River between Washington, DC, and Cumberland, Maryland. Other than where the Towpath's surface was interrupted by locks (elevators that lifted boats up and down to the next canal level), it was flat. Gray squirrels, none of them who could speak as far as I could discern, scurried across or alongside the dirt and stone path, iridescent green mallards and their mottled-brown mates floated serenely, and dreaded Canada geese pecked at green leaves as well as at yellow and red flowers as they waddled near the river's edge.

The race consisted of two laps of 13.1 miles each and occurred in a park that was open to bikers, walkers, and runners who were not competing in the marathon. Based on my prior marathons in which I finished each mile in the neighborhood of ten minutes or so and accounting for the loss of speed and endurance during my two-year absence from marathon running, I optimistically ran the first 20 miles of the Potomac River Run Marathon at a 10:15 pace. David joined me at the beginning of the second 13.1 lap. Encouraging me at every step, he ran next to me. By mile 22, I was fading fast. After invoking all my mental strength, I lightened my physical load by tossing my water vest onto the ground. David picked it up and carried it. About 20 feet from the finish line, he veered off to my right. I finished in 4:42:41. Although my time was my worst ever at this distance, I reminded myself that the minimum standard for 70-74-year-old women to qualify for the 2016 Boston Marathon was 4:55:00. I had more than 12 minutes to spare.

Nothing in life is a sure thing, but I thought that my registration for the Boston Marathon would be accepted.

A Move to an Almost Perfect Running Setting

In spring 2014, David decided that he would retire from high-school teaching in a year. This retirement would be his third. His first had been from a research institute, where he worked for 20 years and the second from the university in the Deep South, where he taught for six years. No longer wedded to Reisterstown after June 2015, we planned to relocate.

David urged consideration of a move to the northern Arizona city of Flagstaff. The area was a running Mecca with many positives. The elevation there is 7,000 feet. Such a rise above sea level is golden for runners. A common belief is that high altitude produces physiological adaptations that improve oxygen-transport systems and enhance sea-level racing performances. The area's majestic forests of Ponderosa pines and miles and miles of suburban and urban trails lure fitness-centric visitors and permanent residents. The weather accommodates outdoor running through much of the year. Summer temperatures are mild, rarely rising above 80 degrees. On the minus side, snowfall in Flagstaff during the winter season is on average 100 inches.

To test the waters, or rather the altitude, we traveled out west in August 2014. Most days we giggled as we fantasized about running for five fast seconds alongside elite racers the likes of the Halls—Ryan, a two-time Olympic marathoner, and Sara, a former US cross-country champion. We gawked at their home during our tour of an under-construction development of yellowish-brown, sage-green, and ecru houses. The community's model home was about 200 feet from the Halls' front door, and the salesperson took pains to point out their residence. Their dusty car was parked outside, but we saw neither hide nor hair of either of them. At least, they could have taken out the trash while we spied on them.

Our time in Flagstaff began the same way each day of our stay. Around 6:00 a.m., we loped along one of two earthen trails bordering our hotel. Yellowish cutie-pie prairie dogs greeted us, barking enthusiastically as we passed their holes inconveniently located smack dab in the middle of each trail. The critters' heads moving up and down evoked the arcade game Whack a Mole. Adorable initially, these broad-faced rodents with short legs and fuzzy tails lost their allure after a few days. The barking became annoying. I wanted them to get out of my way.

We enjoyed dining out and attending entertainment events in and around Flagstaff. We ate our way through an array of restaurants offering items such as pizza, Indian curries, Chinese noodles, Mexican enchiladas, and American roasted chicken. We strolled through regional museums and fidgeted during music events as we waited to applaud performers whose names were unfamiliar to us.

Despite its many assets, Flagstaff was not the place for us. We were age-group runners who would have certainly profited from living and running at high elevation, but we were essentially East-Coast folks who embraced life as we knew it—colonial houses with white exteriors and black shutters, hot and muggy summer days, and proximity to my family. We needed the Baltimore-Washington area's thousands of restaurants offering almost every imaginable cuisine, live theaters aplenty, scores of music venues featuring famous performers, and hundreds of museums celebrating life in the region and in the nation and beyond.

Several months later, we decided to have a house built in New Freedom, Pennsylvania. A chief lure of the new location was that there was no state tax on retirement income, which would be the source of 90 percent of our cash flow. Another attraction was the town's proximity to the Maryland border; as such, it was only 25 miles from the homes of three of my sisters. Additionally, our new house was only eight-tenths of a primarily downhill mile to the relatively flat Northern Central Railroad (NCR) Trail. Finally, our house was surrounded by hilly residential streets with light vehicular traffic. We could alternate running settings easily.

To our amazement, when we put our house on the market in June 2015, it sold in six days. Unfortunately, our new residence in New Freedom would not be ready for another six weeks. After weighing our options, we placed our belongings in a storage facility and moved temporarily into one of the largest units of a nearby extended-stay hotel, where we shared a single bathroom with a single sink and sat on a queen-sized bed as we ate meals on old-school television trays that we purchased from a local Walmart. During this time, we drove to the NCR Trail at least thrice weekly to run. We joined a nearby fitness club where David led me through strengthening and flexibility routines twice a week and where I attempted once again to learn how to swim. All that I gained from the pool experience was an infection that required that I take antibiotics for two weeks.

The settlement date on our New Freedom house was July 31, 2015. Three months after we moved in, David and I hoped to run the October 2015 Steamtown Marathon, a third time for me and a first for him. We traveled to Scranton, Pennsylvania, to check the course, which had changed a bit since I had last run the race. We were naïve. Ordering window treatments, selecting stones for landscaping, and selecting paint colors left us with insufficient time to train. We had already registered for the race. We requested and received a partial refund. Better than losing all of our money, we agreed.

Bird Phobia, Begone!

Living and running in New Freedom was like existence in an aviary. Birds were everywhere, so many that David purchased a field guide and binoculars. Crows, like huge moving black clouds, often darkened the sky as far as we could see. Red-shouldered hawks perched almost every morning on the branches of maples that lined the western side of our backyard. At times, one of them dove to the ground and picked up its still wriggling prey, probably a field mouse, and dropped the creature to the earth to kill it or stun it before it became the meal du jour. These same hawks occasionally thrust their chests out, extended their talons, and battled with other birds that dared to invade their territory. Gray and white mockingbirds, like kamikazes, zoomed almost directly toward the north-facing window of my second-floor office. At what seemed like the last minute, they, their shadows trailing them, landed noisily on the eave several feet above the window. From time to time, a Great Blue Heron leaped from the stream near where the hawks roosted. Startled whenever one of these lanky birds soared, I squealed each time in wonder as I stared at its majesty.

The abundance of all of these birds was problematic for me. I had feared such creatures since I was four years old. Like each of my sisters, I received, on Easter Day 1950, a live yellow peep. Inadvertently, I stepped on mine and squashed the life out of it. I was so traumatized that, oddly, I developed a bird phobia that was later reinforced after I saw Alfred Hitchcock's *The Birds*, a 1963 horror-suspense movie focusing on unexplained bird attacks.

Contradicting this fear was my affinity for hummingbirds. Maybe I admired them because they were so elusive and uncatchable. From inside our New Freedom home, I stared at these visitors who appeared annually in June or July and stayed until autumn. My admiration of this tiny marvel of nature was on prominent display in our morning room where two 20" x 26" color photographs of ruby-throated hummingbirds hung. David and I had purchased the pictures in 2013 when we glimpsed them on the wall of a New Mexico coffee shop during a quick morning meal of steaming coffee and freshly baked, still warm, strawberry muffins. We were visiting David's older brother Phil, a Presbyterian minister and retired Air-Force major, who lived in Socorro, New Mexico. During our stay, we spent an entire day at Basque del Apache National Wildlife Refuge, a preserve with thousands of hummingbirds. A haven for them and a heaven for me!

After our first summer in New Freedom, David and I decided to ramp up our efforts to attract hummingbirds to our backyard. We gave our landscaper marching orders: plant flowers that these feisty birds could not resist—purple coral bells, blue delphinium, and pink bleeding hearts. The pièce de résistance was a black-hawthorn tree. These floras became magnets not only for hummingbirds but also for colorful butterflies such as bright-orange and black monarchs, eastern-tail blues, and red-spotted purples as well as wasps and bumble bees. We upped the ante by hanging bottled nectar on the tree. Also, we hung baskets of fragrant lantana plants with yellow, orange, white, and red florets on a stand on our deck. We placed a second bottle of nectar near the lantana. Once a few ruby-throated hummingbirds discovered these reliable sources of nourishment, they partook many times daily. To our delight, they would return to our yard and deck year after year.

Constant exposure to birds reduced my fear of them. I began to yearn to touch their glossy feathers as they flew near me as I ran. I hoped that some would land on my arms or on my hands or on my shoulders. Sometimes I believed that, for an instant as I sped along, I caught the air and ascended with them.

THE LONELINESS OF SOLO RUNNING

Because I had moved so far away, running with Margaret was impractical. Even had I lived closer to her, our running together would have come to an end. After running from her childhood through her early 60s, she succumbed to an injury that prohibited weight-bearing exercise. She stopped running and devoted most of her fitness time to biking, often covering more than 1,000 miles monthly during spring, summer, and autumn.

About a year after the move to New Freedom, David was felled by a stress fracture, and I was on my own as a runner. Motivational problems surfaced. I struggled to force myself outdoors. Seeking resolution, I began to read about ways to energize myself. I discovered self-hypnosis for running. As recommended in a book on the topic, I connected with the environment at the outset of my solo runs. I gazed at the sky, the trees, and the animals. I relished the weather in all its forms—rainy, windy, snowy, and other variations.

During the first few miles of these solo runs, I engaged in a conversation with my body during which I listened closely. My breathing told me whether I was inhaling and exhaling appropriately. I relaxed my shoulders when my shadow revealed that I was hunching. Quickly, I adjusted my stride whenever I heard my right foot drag as it often did. I listened to the message that my body sent about how I was dressed. If I became overheated or cold at the end of a half-mile, it told me to wear less or more clothing the next time that I ran in such conditions. If my feet slid forward in my shoes, I stopped, tightened the laces, and retied my shoes. I tuned into my pace—increasing or decreasing it based on the run's objectives.

I thought that solo running satisfied me. However, impulsively one morning, I drove to Druid Hill Park, a 36-mile drive from New Freedom. For old time's sake, I looped the reservoir. I planned to circle it several times and then return home. The second time around, I encountered a tall, wiry African-American man with dreadlocks pulled back into a ponytail. He appeared to be in his late 30s. He ran up next to me and began to chat. I was not surprised. Frequently, Park regulars began conversations with strangers.

"I'm Liam," he said. His full name was Liam Dowd Murphy, I later learned. Such an Irish name? We ran around the reservoir a few more times. During one of our circles, I glimpsed shimmering hummingbirds beating their wings against the backdrop of abundant trees so rapidly that they became blurs of red, emerald, gold, gray, and white. Awestruck, I stopped for a few seconds to stare. He followed suit.

After a few more loops, Liam and I agreed to meet on the following Thursday at midday at the reservoir. A few weeks after we began our mid-week runs, he offered to meet me at Ernst Park in New Freedom on Saturdays while David was injured. The trip, he explained, would be an easy one for him, taking no more than 45 minutes. By 9:00 a.m., he was usually waiting for me.

During our second run from Ernst Park, Liam suggested, "Let's race to the red posts near the Steam-into-History gift shop. I'm going to give you a head start." Before I could respond, he yelled, "Let's rock and roll." I squealed, "The shop's more than a mile away. I already know that you're going to beat me." Smiling, he responded, "Maybe. Maybe not."

Huffing and puffing, I looked on my left as we ran northward on the Trail past a housing development with forest-green, cocoa-brown, and dove-gray homes. At this point, my eyes almost always drifted to the right. I shuddered as I stared at a poster in the window of an old two-story puke-colored house that predated the development. The poster screamed, "Face It! Abortion kills a person." An angelic infant's face drove this point home.

Breathless when we reached the gift shop, I stopped for a few seconds as did he. Smoke hissed from a steam locomotive—a replica of a brightly painted red, yellow, and black 1860's train that, in the present day, transported tourists a few miles north on a now-defunct railroad line and then returned them to the gift shop. After we ran another quarter of a mile, Liam and I both looked up at a seven-foot free-standing black street clock that had no hands. We slowly jogged about 100 feet north past the Rail Trail Café and the New Freedom Railroad Museum, located next to one another on our left and past a bright red "Party Caboose" on the right that could be rented for children's parties.

I told Liam that I needed to stop at the ladies' room. Patiently, he stood outside. I admired his bladder control. As he waited, he was not alone. Tied on wooden railings immediately outside the restroom doors, runners' and walkers' dogs sat quietly and calmly. When I exited the ladies' room, they barked loudly. One or two of them growled at me. Maybe Liam was a dog whisperer.

As we ran, Liam and I confided in one another. He told me about the ups and downs of his ten-year relationship with Jim, a man he met while they were both sophomores at the City College of New York. When Liam accepted a position as an engineer at Black and Decker, located near Baltimore, his partner reluctantly joined him. Jim relished New York City's cultural and restaurant scene and found Baltimore an inferior landscape. Liam and Jim had recently moved into a waterfront luxury condo in a 24-floor tower located in Baltimore's up-and-coming Locust-Point neighborhood. When we stopped to consume energy gels, Liam showed me photos on his phone of his Scandinavian-influenced home replete with beech floors, beige walls, cream-colored upholstery, plentiful natural light, and abundant plants. Although we had run with one another for a few months, Liam never offered to introduce me to his partner nor invited me to visit his condo. Following his lead, I never introduced him to David nor invited him to my home filled with art collected during my travels—treasures such as a green-jade carving of a cabbage, red and gold antique Mongolian battle flags, and a white-jade carving of Chinese flying horses that David toted halfway across the world in a Shanghai-purchased knock-off Versace suitcase that fell apart on the first day that we returned home from a month-long trip. Liam never saw our shrine to Bryan—photographs of our son at all ages and stages as well as a poster promoting a movie that our son co-wrote—that David had meticulously positioned on our basement walls.

During our first few runs, I moaned incessantly about the pain of my ouster from my chancellorship and the anguish of selling my house in Phillips Fields. Liam listened patiently the first few times that I raised these topics. One morning, though, he stopped running, it seemed in mid stride, and looked into my eyes. "T. J., you need to stop talking about this stuff. You lost your job years ago. You didn't think something like that could happen to you. Your sense of yourself as this always victorious person crumbled. But both of us know that you had been thinking about moving on within a year or two anyway because you were bored there."

He paused. Then he added, "The house in Phillips Fields was sold years ago. Again, if you're honest with yourself, you'd admit that you didn't like living there. You told me that the little boys who lived next door to you kicked balls into your garage door and dented it and that these same kids kicked balls into your car and dimpled it. You whined that some of your neighbors' front lawns looked terrible. One neighbor even transformed his front yard into a baseball field because he didn't have enough room behind his house for his children to play."

Initially, I was taken aback. Reading my hurt face, gently, he continued, "Live in the moment. In the present. It's okay to learn from the past, but you shouldn't let it harm you forever. You need to move on. Don't waste time lamenting things you can't change."

Shortly thereafter during the run, he surprised me. He praised me. "You're really doing great with your running." I disagreed with him. "No, I'm not. I should be running faster." As I flagellated myself, he abruptly halted. Confused, I stopped as well. He grabbed my hands and stroking them gently, he said, "Stop right now! You're fast enough. That's why you win so many age-group awards."

I argued, "I win because usually I don't have much competition."

Clearly annoyed, he said, "When you have competition, you win most of the time!" Then he embraced me. He pled, "Love yourself."

Then Liam asked, "Do you have your phone with you?" Often, I did not have it with me, but on this day, I carried it inside my sports bra. I removed the paper towel in which I had wrapped it and handed it to him. My phone wallpaper was a photo of me that he had seen a few times. Studying the photograph, he asked, "Tell me again how old you were then." "Nine," I responded. Smiling softly, he said, "You were so cute in that plaid dress that your Mama fastened at the neck with a safety pin because the top button was missing. Your eyes are so innocent and trusting." Then he said, "Be kind to that little girl."

After a minute of quiet, he muttered, "You've often told me how poor your family was. Your mother must have loved you so much. Think about how hard it was for her to come up with the money for that photo."

Liam ran with me on Saturdays for several more months. One Saturday, though, I walked to Ernst Park, and his car was not there. For a few more weeks, I hurried to this location, hoping he would be waiting for me. However, he never reappeared. Only then did I realize that I had no way of communicating with him.

No phone number. No email address. Why had I never asked him for his contact information? Stung by his abandonment and weighed down by self-pity, I ran alone once more.

On a whim, one Thursday a few weeks later, I returned to Druid Hill Park. Maybe I would find Liam there. Sitting on a gray-metal bench was a wizened dark-brown man I had seen rooted to a bench in the past. I told him what Liam looked like and asked the man whether he had seen someone matching the description. With a befuddled look on his face, the man mumbled, "I ain't never seed nobody looking like that. I done seed you, though, out here running alone months ago talking to yourself." He continued, "I thought you was one of the strange folks that is out here."

During a dinner at a Baltimore restaurant, I told David and Bryan about Liam and about my conversation with the old man at the Park. David frowned. I had formed the habit of talking endlessly about people with whom I ran. I had never mentioned Liam. He believed I had run alone during his hiatus.

Impishly, Bryan speculated, "Maybe Liam is a pooka. Your DNA analysis showed that some of your ancestors are Irish. Pookas appear often in Irish folklore. Maybe somehow they crept into your collective unconscious." He chuckled. His green eyes gleamed with amusement.

"What in the world is a pooka?" I asked, miffed. Instantly, he answered, "A trickster or prankster. Puck, the elf, in Shakespeare's *A Midsummer Night's Dream* is a pooka. Harvey, the tall rabbit in that old movie starring Jimmy Stewart, is a pooka. Only Elwood P. Dodd, Stewart's character, can see and hear Harvey." How in the world did Bryan know about this 1950's movie? I barely remembered it.

In hindsight, I should not have been surprised by Bryan's rapid-fire responses. He had an encyclopedic memory. For that reason, he was a prized team member whenever my extended family played fact-based games such as *Jeopardy* and *Trivial Pursuit*. He was such a fount of information that his teams almost always won. As his mother, I beamed when he casually exhibited his command of information.

After I reflected a bit on his answer, I asked, "Are you suggesting that I'm nuts? That Liam is not a real person?"

"Know thyself," Bryan responded. He guffawed. I wanted to strangle him, but instead I opted to cause him minor discomfort. I reached for his long curly ponytail, knowing it was tangled, and raked my fingers through his mane. He squealed, "Ouch!"

If I thought the pain would shut him up, I was wrong. Still laughing loudly, Bryan added, "Maybe Liam is a gorilla." I could not believe that he resurrected this specter from my youth. My sisters had poisoned his mind by telling him about my childhood misadventure with Joanne whenever they could insert this episode into a conversation.

Constant Threats: Dogs, Dogs, Dogs

According to the 2010 US Census, 4,565 people lived in the borough of New Freedom, which occupied all of 2.08 square miles. In 2017, two years after we moved there, the population had grown modestly to 4,685.

Based on my seemingly endless encounters with yapping, snarling, growling, and rampaging canines, I suspected that the town was home to at least twice the number of dogs as people. Many of the borough's canines were unleashed and posed dangers to runners, walkers, and bikers.

I did not have to learn firsthand about how dogs imperiled runners. Decades before I became a runner, David faced off against canines from time to time and unleashed his fury about these encounters when he returned home. Specifically, I remember his anger after a five miler. "Take a look at these pants!" he yelled. After staring a few seconds and seeing nothing awry, I asked, "Aren't those the black Gore-Tex running pants I gave you for Christmas?" At the time, the mid-1980s, clothing produced by this brand was the apex of running attire; the products were waterproof, lightweight, and breathable.

Exasperated, David squawked, "What's different about them?" I looked closely again. "There're holes around the hem." Reddening his left palm by pounding his right fist into it, he responded loudly, "Yes! Yes! Yes! Some damned little dog came from out of nowhere. It growled at me. I growled back at it. Then it ran after me. That mutt meant to bite me, but instead it bit my pant leg. I was so livid I turned around and chased it. It ran toward some of its buddies. Suddenly, a whole bunch of them were on my heels." He paused. "I rushed inside a Seven-Eleven to get away from them."

Some runners were not as fortunate as David was that day. Betsy, a smiling fortyish blonde I met when I first began to run solo on the Trail near New Freedom was one such person. During our first conversation, she told me where she lived and how often she ran. As gesticulations punctuated her sentences, I noticed that she had a phone jammed between her melon-like pink breasts. A canister of pepper spray dangled from her wrist. I stared at the tiny cylinder. Pointing to the spray, she asked, "Are you wondering why I carry this?" I responded, "Yes. There're always people on the Trail. Why do you think you need it?"

She then shared a cautionary tale. Months earlier, she had seen a large gray dog running off leash on the Trail. Given that its owner waded a few feet away in a stream, she paid little attention to the dog although it bared its teeth and snarled as she ran near it. Suddenly, it lunged at her. It latched onto her shoulder, its teeth ripping into her soft flesh. With all her strength, she punched it in the nose, she said. Instead of caring about Betsy, the dog's angry owner yelled, "You hurt my dog." Betsy told me that she countered, "You're darned right I did." The woman leashed the dog and scurried away without offering any assistance. Without a phone with which she could have taken a photo of the dog and its owner and with which she could have phoned someone for help, Betsy rushed two miles home with sticky blood oozing from the ragged gash in her shoulder. She endured a painful series of rabies shots.

I should have carried my phone with me faithfully after this encounter, but I did not always take it with me. I had several excuses. When I stuck it inside my bra, it bruised my skin, leaving a rectangular outline on my chest. Reception was spotty or nonexistent on much of the Trail, so toting it yielded little increased safety unless perhaps I used the phone as a projectile. The likelihood of my capturing images of run-amuck dogs was low. I doubted that I would have the composure to pull the camera out of my bra and snap pictures as Fido came at me.

Betsy's dog experience resonated with me every time that I ran on the streets of New Freedom or on the Trail. Virtually every single day when I left home, I braved a canine gauntlet. If I turned left at the end of the driveway, walked approximately 150 feet, and turned right, I frequently encountered William, a massive black Great Dane wearing a baby-blue collar. He probably weighed over 175 pounds, I guessed, and stood around three feet tall at the shoulder. He looked as though he might be approximately six feet tall when he looked down on me from a stacked-stone raised planter on his family's front lawn. Surrounded by low-growing red blooms and tall bright-purplish flowers with yellow centers during spring and summer months, the majestic dog surveyed his domain—not just his yard but also, his body language suggested, his entire street. Whenever he barked at me in his deep bass voice, my anxiety spiraled.

One morning when William paced like a sentry back and forth, his male human assured me, "He's harmless. We've got a two-year-old girl, and William plays with her all the time." Probably discerning my doubts about his veracity, he added, "Don't be intimidated by his size. He won't hurt you. We've got an electric fence, and he won't go through it." A few days later, however, William stood smack dab in the middle of the street. Either the owner had forgotten to turn on the zapping feature of the fence, or William was unfazed by the current. As soon as I saw him, I U-turned and walked slowly away.

On days when William was not outdoors, I ventured past his house. On one such morning, I complacently trotted by his house secure in the knowledge that I would enjoy dog-free running for at least five minutes or so. Suddenly, two heavily salivating, loudly growling German shepherds that I had never seen before burst from behind a red-brick house that I passed a few minutes beyond William's house. No humans appeared to be around. No visible fence separated them from me. I made no assumptions about the existence of an electric fence. I slowed to a walk and prayed that the beasts would not chase me and rip my flesh from my bones. They stopped at the edge of their yard. I never followed this route again. No more Williams. No more German shepherds.

A half-mile beyond the red-brick house, often three white maltipoos that probably weighed eight or nine pounds each yapped as they maniacally sprinted back and forth on their lawn. They amused me, for they appeared to believe that I should be afraid of them. Usually, their owner, a smiling middle-aged woman, was outdoors or standing in her doorway when I ran by. When she caught my eye, she often waved.

On days when I turned right at the end of my driveway—in the direction away from William's house, I walked uphill about 150 yards before I encountered a lustrous steel-gray standard schnauzer whose bushy snout quivered as he snarled and dashed around the border of his yard. I knew his gender immediately. I had developed the habit of checking canine genitalia automatically as soon as I encountered said animal. The dog startled me the first time that he pounced from behind a tree. When I saw a red collar around his neck and the creature remained on its lawn, I assumed that an invisible electric fence was in place. Over time, I assumed the schnauzer would become accustomed to me. Faint hope! The dog saw me thrice weekly sometimes, but it ran around in circles nonetheless and barked ferociously each time.

Shortly after I passed the schnauzer, I faced off against a brown boxer, a female, that often charged from behind a bush whenever I walked or ran by. Startled by her sudden appearance the first few times that I encountered her, I was so rattled that I crossed to the opposite side of the street. I could swear that the boxer was a tad amused by my response to her. As time passed, I stopped crossing over, for the dog remained on her lawn.

After a half-mile, I came upon a pink-collared dog that yapped incessantly as she followed me along the periphery of her front lawn. A white, gray, and brown wire-haired fox terrier, she looked almost exactly like Asta, Nick and Nora Charles' pet dog in the 1930s' and 1940s' *The Thin Man* detective-comedy movies. Initially, I worried that the terrier might dash onto the street. Then I noticed a Dog Watch sign, signaling an electric fence, fastened to a metal post.

As I was about to move on, a fiftyish brunette woman walked slowly to a mailbox and pulled down its lip. I introduced myself. She responded, "I'm Carol." I gushed, "Your dog is so adorable. What's her name?" She said, "Gracie. She's got lots of admirers. The UPS guys give her treats all the time." She added, "But don't let her cuteness fool you. She's quite a handful." I resisted the urge to tell her that some mail carriers and delivery people used pet snacks to curry favor with dogs, cute and not so cute, to reduce the likelihood of attacks.

On some subsequent mornings, Gracie sprinted to her electric border, romped around energetically, and greeted me loudly. On other mornings, she stared coldly and gave me the silent treatment. There never seemed to be a middle ground. Regardless of her behavior, I blew kisses in her direction.

Usually, I saw no other dogs in the remaining tenth of a mile from Gracie's yard to the Trail. One morning, though, I ran about 30 feet or so from Gracie's house when a dark-brown teacup maltipoo in attack mode burst from an open back door. The petite canine was seemingly bent on mayhem. I grabbed the dog, which wriggled in my hands, in much the way that I had seen fish at the ends of reels attempt to escape capture. She bit at me. I carried it with its head far enough forward that its tiny teeth could not reach my hand, knocked on the door from whence the tiny dog had made its exit onto the street, and deposited it into a surprised woman's outstretched hands. I complained, "Your dog was on the street, and it attacked me." With a look that combined embarrassment and amusement, the woman said, "She's a nipper. She often goes for us." The "us" included, I assumed, the two blonde elementary-school-age children peeking from behind her.

I knew from my encounter with the squirrel years ago in Druid Hill Park that occasionally I possessed an uncanny ability to comprehend animal thought and utterances. One day I stopped to talk with Nancy, a fortyish blonde woman with a corral alongside the Trail where her two black quarter horses and her golden Shetland pony spent most of their days munching green grass growing among dark-brown clumps of their own manure. A small red stable at the most distant edge of the property was their nighttime abode. On a fence, several signs urged, "Don't Feed the Horses."

As she and I chatted, a pair of black Doberman pinschers with rust markings above their eyes and on their throats, chests, legs, and feet sidled up next to her. One was slightly taller than the other. I knew the breed. During my youth, Dobermans had been, in Baltimore's poorest neighborhoods, young African-American males' canines of choice. These dogs inspired as much fear in me then as pit bulls did later. Like a proud mother, Nancy unabashedly boasted about her Dobermans' intelligence, their loyalty, and their obedience. Although I had read about this breed's strengths, including their gentleness, fear froze me as she chirped, "They do their job of guarding this corral." She continued, "See how friendly they are." I did not believe a single syllable that she uttered about their virtues. I wondered whether she might be living in some alternative universe. What I detected was not even remotely similar to her description of her dogs. On the heels of this thought, the taller Doberman who was closer to me than was the other, gave me a side eye, slowly moved his mouth revealing sharp, pointy teeth, and uttered guttural sounds perversely at odds with what Nancy said. Looking me in the eyes, he muttered menacingly, "Be glad she's here. Otherwise, we'd tear your throat out."

For weeks after my introduction to the Dobermans, my runs near the horse corral were uneventful. Then one morning as I finished a run, about 200 feet south of the corral, an unleashed black and white female Australian shepherd with white-tipped ears bounded along toward me. I recognized the animal. I had seen her in the past on a leash. No humans were in sight that day. I cringed. "Ignore me," I prayed. I continued along at the same cool-down pace at which I had been running before the dog appeared. I uttered a sigh of relief as it silently trotted by without appearing to notice me.

A few weeks later, I encountered the same canine again. The Trail was eerily quiet. However, this time the Australian shepherd did not ignore me. Instead, it aggressively barked. I stopped running as the dog, true to its breed, seemed to want to herd me and force me to remain in one place. As I wondered how to handle the mess in which I found myself, a woman's voice pierced the dog's barks. Through slim openings in dense maple trees, I saw a young-looking woman with a brunette ponytail standing on the porch of a red-roofed house located about 200 feet above the Trail. I assumed that she was the person I had seen walking the dog in the past. Repeatedly, she cupped her hands to her mouth and yelled loudly in an authoritarian voice, "Marian, you better get back here." The dog ignored her. Finally, after at least five threats, the dog obeyed and ran in the woman's direction much to my relief.

When it rains, it pours. Trite but often true. A few weeks later, I encountered another off-leash canine near this same spot. Earlier that day I had overcome exhaustion, primarily tied to my being on my feet nonstop during 90 percent of my waking hours for the two immediately preceding days during which I baked desserts such as chocolate-walnut cookies, vanilla pound cake, lemon-meringue pie, and other sweet treats and cooked savory dishes such as chicken empanadas, North-Carolina barbecued pork, and beef short ribs. My youngest sister had suckered me into hosting a game party during which my hypercompetitive sisters and my visiting niece's family as well as David, Bryan, and I would vie against one another playing bingo, *Pokeno*, and the like.

Initially, my youngest sister pretended my hosting the game party was optional. In an email to me, on which she copied all of my siblings and my niece, she introduced the idea and then ended with the words "No pressure. Your choice."

In the middle of cooking for the party, I squeezed in a speed workout that consisted of a warm-up mile, eight 400s, and a cool-down mile. I chose the section of the Trail near where I had encountered the dog Marian both times because its surface was asphalt for the most part and fairly flat. Usually, a few bikers and walkers were in the area, and two houses, whose occupants I had never seen outdoors, were nearby.

Suddenly, as I finished one of the 400s, a hulking male German shepherd, his blackish coat standing at attention, rushed toward me. I had seen him a minute or so earlier as he dashed on a path about 300 feet above me. That the animal would descend did not occur to me. But there he was next to me, growling and lunging. I did not know what to do. Unlike the city-park squirrel that I met years earlier and the Doberman, the German shepherd did not transmit any thoughts that I could hear. I prayed for rescue. However, the cavalry did not miraculously gallop over a crest. I was on my own. If I ran, I might provoke the dog. He might see me as prey, easily catch me, and tear me apart. My first thought was that I should walk slowly away from him. I took a few tentative steps. This slight movement agitated the dog, and his aggression heightened. He bared his yellowish teeth, exposing his pink gums. Steaming colorless spittle flowed from the corners of his mouth. As my mind raced, the dog circled me slowly. I remained absolutely still. I forced myself to look away from him for fear that he might see my staring as a challenge. After what seemed like an eternity, the dog lost interest and loped away. After I could hear the pads of his paws no longer, I turned slowly around to make sure that he had indeed run off.

For a month or so, I avoided the Trail. When I returned, I never saw the German shepherd again.

TRAIL CREATURES ABOUNDING: GNATS, CATS, RODENTS, A FOX, AND A BEAR

One August morning, Mother Nature handed me a weather gift—temperatures in the 70s, cool breezes, blessed rain, and a cloudy sky. What a respite from the 90-degree temperatures, 90-percent humidity, still air, and high UV levels that were the norm at this time of year.

Because of these conditions, most flying creatures had abandoned the Trail. No butterflies with blue-tipped wings glided a hair's distance from my nose. No mosquitoes satisfied their hunger by gulping my blood. No horse flies such as the one that bit me a few weeks earlier and whose attack left three dark marks and a weeklong itch ambushed me. The weight of water caused these creatures' wings to stick together, and the wind caused them to use more-than-normal energy to flutter or soar.

After I ran the first mile, black clouds of gnats that not even rain could scatter encircled my face like a veil and stayed with me. They attempted to establish colonies within my ear canals even though I ran with earphones. They tried to fly into my eyes, but I wore sunglasses even in the rain that prevented access. Donning them was a running habit regardless of the weather. Also, the glasses hid the bags under my eyes.

Usually, I avoided dealing death to Mother Nature's progeny, but enough was enough. Channeling President Barack Obama, who famously squashed a fly in an amazing display of eye-hand coordination during a June 2009 CNBC interview that became an Internet sensation, I slapped my hands together and terminated one single gnat among the hordes of them. After ending the creature's life, pride in my coordination suffused me for half a second. Then I admitted to myself that I had just gotten lucky. The swarm was so thick that had my eye-hand coordination truly been good, I would have been responsible for the "transition" of at least two or three critters. I laughed out loud. "Transition?" Why do some people use this euphemism to signify death?

Although the gnats distracted me, I was hyperconscious of my aloneness. Only two or three bikers moved cautiously past me. I was startled to see them. Bikers did not usually risk their limbs or their equipment by venturing out in rainy weather.

While gangs of gnats were annoyances, creatures not of this species had an opposite impact. Cats that I encountered fascinated me. One of these was a brown and white bushy-tailed feline, whose gender I could not determine, haughtily strolling along one Sunday next to two teenagers, a boy and a girl, and a man and woman I assumed were their parents. I had always believed that cats were too independent to be trained to walk off leash, or even on leash, with humans. The girl said to the cat, "Stay with us. Don't go over there." "There" was a narrow metal plank parallel to the Trail with an approximately two-foot-wide space on each side. About ten feet below the rail was swirling water. The cat ignored the girl's warning and, full of grace, it hopped onto the plank and moved the front and rear legs on its left side simultaneously and then the legs on the right side, creating the impression that it glided. It was clear that the cat was not walking with the family; the family was walking with it.

During another run, on a hot day, I passed a white Victorian house where two tuxedo cats of unknown gender lounged on a weedy lawn littered with tiny glass shards, bits of paper, and random debris. Initially, the felines were so still that I thought they were lawn ornaments. Then one of them raised an eyelid, revealing a green iris, and sneered. Contemptuously, it meowed,

"Only a stupid human like you would be running outside in 95-degree weather and 90-percent humidity."

These two cats reminded me of another tuxedo cat, a solitary one of unknown gender, I often encountered a mile or so north of the Victorian house. This feline stared at me, its green-gold eyes unblinking. Sometimes, it sauntered alongside the Trail, but most often it parked itself like a black-and-white Sphinx under some bushes and observed me and the world at large with indifferent eyes. Even when I stopped, wiped the lens of my phone with the hem of my running skirt, and snapped a photo of it, the creature moved not a muscle.

Other animals roamed the Trail as well. Hurdling or sprinting or just plain scurrying, gray squirrels ranged in all seasons and often caused me to stop short when they dashed across my path. Visible during all seasons except winters, sprightly chipmunks, reddish-brown with alternating dark and light stripes, often hurried homeward to their hidden burrows. Now and then, brownish-grayish furry groundhogs lumbered into creeping vines beneath maple and oak trees. Once in a while, a lithe red fox stared aslant at me as it, bushy tail trailing, vanished into shrubs and undergrowth.

Domesticated animals (other than cats, whose willfulness excluded them, in my feline-loving mind, from this category) also lived near the Trail. From time to time, I ran so close to a grazing herd of dark-brown cows that I thought I could hear them chewing lush dark-green grass. Once, I glimpsed 20 to 25 black and white pygmy goats leaping gracefully over decaying tree stumps inside a fenced area near a gray colonial house and a reddish barn that were adjacent to the Trail. Such synchronization.

On the day I saw the goats, I ran about a mile north toward a bridge that arched the Trail. Its gray-stone supports were streaked with a lime-colored substance. Whenever I reached this spot, I wondered whether a family of jaundiced trolls, yellow eyes aglow, had escaped from Scandinavian folklore and found this bridge, clawed upward over rocks and twigs, and then spewed bile below. Completing the scene were gold-brown grasses sprouting from rocks' fissures—like lustrous chestnut horses' manes. Clumps of black vegetation hung like sleeping bats from the bridge's underbelly.

Most of the time, the only sounds I heard in this area were rumbling and vrooming cars and trucks overhead. On one morning, however, unfamiliar sounds, grunts and slapping noises, interrupted my thoughts. I looked backwards and saw a gigantic dark creature, the likes of which I had never seen on the Trail, thundering toward me. I sprinted away. But it gained ground. For a moment, it halted and rubbed its belly against several trees. Terrified, I darted into the woods and hid behind a stand of trees. It charged along the Trail, bumping against the sides of rocks and bushes. As it passed me, it opened its maw, oozing a gooey greenish substance and making loud deep-throated sounds.

Ten minutes later as I, trembling, returned to the Trail and tentatively ran homeward, I saw, on the horizon, a man in a bright-orange jacket striding comfortably toward me. He had to have passed the beast.

Shaking, I rushed toward him. Breathlessly, I asked, "How did you avoid the bear?"

With a puzzled look on his lined face, the man asked, "What bear?"

"The one that was on the Trail not long ago."

He wrinkled his face. "I didn't see a bear."

He asked, "How close were you to this thing?"

"I saw it from a distance of about 100 feet," I murmured.

After searching my face for what seemed like eons, he said, "Bears are rarely seen in this part of the state." He cleared his throat and continued, "I saw a large pile of brown leaves and branches that were somehow attached to one another. Blasts of wind carried them along the Trail. From a distance, I suppose the bundle might have looked like a running animal."

"Oh," I responded.

I felt the blood rush to my face. My brown skin masked the flush of my embarrassment. In my mind, I heard my sisters' raucous laughter as they chimed, "Another gorilla."

Good Vibes from Most Trail People

Given that the population in New Freedom and the surrounding environs was approximately 96 percent white, the homogeneity of the people on the Trail was predictable. I was the "other" but became such a regular in this setting that few people seemed surprised to see me.

On weekdays during spring, summer, and early fall, I often ran past women or men walking in ones, communing with nature or communing with their dogs, or walking in twos and threes, often so engrossed in conversations that they, oblivious to the rest of us nearby, spread across the entire breadth of the path with their bodies and their dogs' bodies. Sometimes, I ran by young mothers pushing their rosy-cheeked babies and toddlers in strollers. More often, white-haired men zoomed by me on their road bikes, gears whirring. Less often, sets of men and women on cruisers dawdled by me. Now and then, youngish runners alone with their thoughts or their music outpaced me, leaving me wishing that I were faster. On weekends, similar collections of people moved along, but in greater numbers, up and down the Trail.

Of the people I encountered in this setting, two of the more anomalous were a once-seen pair of teenage boys in Amish attire (straw hats, white shirts, and black pants held up with black suspenders) bustling, it seemed, with a purpose one summer morning near the Mason-Dixon Line, originally the boundary between Maryland and Pennsylvania and the dividing line before the Civil War between slave states to the south and free states to the north. Although Pennsylvania was home to one of the largest groups of Amish citizens in the US, I was startled nonetheless to see the boys. They did not greet me, and I said nothing to them.

There were two persons I encountered like clockwork on the Trail. Then suddenly I saw them no more. Without an apparent purpose, Roger—a sallow, scruffy, blankly grinning man with missing upper front teeth—rambled a little over a mile south from the borough of Railroad, Pennsylvania, home to 248 people in 2018, to the Rail Trail Café, where he sat at one of the outdoor tables regardless of the season, and then strolled back to Railroad. His few utterances sounded like mumbo jumbo.

The other person was Sandra. She was the only African-American person I regularly encountered. Unmarried, she lived alone, she told me, in a development in the borough of Glen Rock, one of the last places where I thought that people of my race resided until I learned that it was home to more African Americans than was New Freedom. In Glen Rock, 1,944 people lived as of July 1, 2018. Of the inhabitants then, 95.30 percent were White, and 2.77 percent were African American. The rest of the population was made up of other races.

Usually, on Saturdays or Sundays, Sandra parked her car in Railroad and plodded approximately four miles south from there to Freeland (one and a half miles into Maryland), and then she reversed direction and returned to her car. Wide smiles were the norm whenever I saw her. She was agitated and tearful, however, one Sunday morning. More than $100 in cash that she had stashed in her jacket pocket had fallen out as she walked, she told me. I volunteered to help her search although I believed that this effort would be futile. Like camouflage, the green currency would have blended with the grass. Running slowly as I looked downward for about a half-mile, I could have easily bumped into someone because I paid so little attention to what was at eye level. Miraculously, in a patch of grass a few inches off the Trail, I glimpsed a wad of bills. Gleefully, I picked up the cash, ran back toward her, and handed the money to her. Her eyes shone. Her smile returned. She hugged me.

For more than a year, I interrupted my runs and chatted with Sandra most weekends about mundane topics such as the achievement of her dream of owning a detached house in "PA," her reference to the state of Pennsylvania. Like many native Marylanders, she had migrated to the area because of the relatively low cost of housing and the low crime rate. Usually, during our brief conversations, she talked about how she was redecorating her house and about the fun that she had at northern-Maryland karaoke joints and night clubs. Then, like Roger, she was no longer a Trail regular.

While pleasant regulars such as Roger and Sandra were the norm on the Trail, strangers were also usually friendly. One such person, a slow-walking graybeard I had never seen before, surprised me when, after wobbling toward a bench, he wiped browning leaves and dried gray mud from the seat, gingerly sat down, and thrust his hand out. "Here," he offered. "Want some?" He held an unopened bottle of eerily cyan-blue sports liquid. "It's cold," he added. I smiled at his generosity and responded, "Thanks, but I'm fine. I've got cold water." Actually, my water was tepid. Other than during my first half marathon, I never accepted drinks, even unopened beverages, from strangers.

On yet another day, I came upon two white-haired women—one who appeared to be in her 70s and the other in her 50s. The older woman waved me down. Yielding to politeness, I stopped. They introduced themselves as mother and daughter. Each had eyes the color of aquamarine. A leashed miniature poodle, white and fluffy, yapped alongside them. Smiling, the older woman observed, "You're not breathing hard." Perhaps because it was so visible from where we stood, she pointed out a white church with a steeple visible through the green of the trees. "I've been a member there all my life," she proclaimed. Next, she pointed to a neat white building about 150 feet from the church. "My family has owned that house for over a hundred years," she rambled. I wanted to continue my run, but I did not want to be rude, so I stood there as the mother next talked about the magic of turmeric and about exercises that she had been doing to improve her balance. Finally, I said, "I'll let you ladies continue your walk." But she did not let me go. She asked, "Do you know that from this point you're going to have to run 600 feet uphill to reach the center of New Freedom?" I assured her that I had run the route many times and was not concerned about the distance. I escaped their friendliness and continued my run.

On another day, as I was nearing the end of a ten-mile run, a near-empty silver-and-red foil packet slipped from my hand. It was tacky with chocolate gel that I had sipped for an hour and a half. I stopped to pick the packet up, causing a chain reaction of sorts. A biker was immediately behind me, and he stopped pedaling to avoid running into me. I apologized, "Sorry. Can't be a litter bug." Good naturedly, he said, "No problem." I began to run again. He was biking slowly and was still behind me. After a few feet, I dropped the packet yet another time. "Gee! Sorry again," I said. This time the biker offered, "You can put it in the trash compartment of my saddle." I replied, "It's really sticky." He smiled and said, "I don't mind." He was probably glad to be rid of me.

As soon as he pedaled away, I began to run again. I had about a half-mile left before I reached my objective. I heard footsteps behind me. When I looked over my shoulder, I saw a young man with a brown ponytail and hairy legs catching up with me. I threw down the gauntlet. I said aloud, "You're not going to pass me." He replied, "I probably won't. I'm on my seventh mile." I countered, "I'm ending my tenth mile." I sprinted. Maybe someday, I would be able to tamp down my competitiveness. Not that day. Heartily, the young man laughed. I chuckled. I exited the Trail and began my cool-down walk home.

The good vibes on the Trail were not limited to runners, walkers, and bikers. One morning as I ran south into Maryland, a man in a tan floppy gardening hat and a shirt emblazoned with Maryland Department of Natural Resources moved along the edges of the Trail on a yellow trimmer-mower. Such excellent maintenance was typical on both the Maryland and Pennsylvania sections of the Trail. Not only were grass and overgrowth cut regularly, but also whenever rain formed ruts, a crew materialized to fill in potentially ankle-spraining spaces with a silky substance that was a surrogate for soil. Whenever trees fell and blocked sections of the Trail, a crew appeared almost instantly to cut the branches into uniform lengths and stack them in the neatest of piles off the path.

The man in the floppy hat mowed until I neared him. Then he turned off the equipment and waited a minute or so for me to dash by before he restarted it. I apologized. "Sorry I'm interrupting your work." He smiled and said, "This Trail's here for your use. I'm happy to be out here making it a good place for you to run." Over my shoulder, I shouted, "Have a good day." He responded, "You have an even better one."

From time to time, though, my being different dissipated the good feelings I usually associated with the Trail. One of the times I felt most like an alien occurred when I ran near a red-haired teenage girl with pallid skin. On a hot, sunny day, she penetrated my bubble. The physical stereotype of an Irish lass, she was part of a trio of females that included a younger red-headed girl and a golden-haired woman. An off-leash puppy, a golden retriever, frolicked alongside. I wondered how the children and the woman, eerily pale, had managed to avoid reddening or tanning from the brutal sun. Every time I stepped outside, my skin darkened. David marveled. "The rich get richer," he said when I returned home browner and browner after each run.

The teenage girl seemed a bit on edge when I passed her when she was with the other girl and the woman. After I made a U-turn, I saw her running alone while the other members of the group walked far behind her. When she saw me, her frightened-looking face became even whiter. Almost frantically, I thought, she stared over her shoulder. No doubt she had been acculturated to be afraid of people who looked like me. As these thoughts besieged me, I remembered Bryan's comments about how strangers often feared him because, as he said, "I'm a big Black man." And at 6'4" and 200 pounds, he was. I was consistently described as petite or tiny. My size should intimidate neither adult nor child. My skin had to be the genesis of her consternation. The teenager had no idea that we might share common roots, at least in terms of national origin. Like the vast majority of African Americans, I had inherited European blood from White men who ravished my Black-female ancestors. In my case, as Bryan reminded me when he speculated that Liam was a pooka, the majority of my non-African DNA came from antecedents hailing from the Emerald Isle.

A week or so later, I saw the teenager once more. She ran slowly. The younger girl and the golden-retriever puppy walked behind her. The woman was not with them. As I passed the teenager on her left, she glanced at me, her red ponytail whipping across part of her face. Automatically, I said, "Hi." Politely but disinterestedly, her face conveyed, she muttered, "Hello."

Months later, I became a participant in a scenario that caused me to mull further my role as "the other." When I went out one cool Saturday morning to run nine miles, exhaustion, loyal to a fault, accompanied me. Chill joined us. The first two miles, which I decided to run on the streets of the town, seemed endless. Having forgotten to inhale Albuterol to treat my exercise-induced asthma before I left home, I gulped for air. I indulged in a twenty-second walk break. Just as difficult as breathing that morning was my finding a reason to be upbeat as I struggled. What I had learned about self-hypnosis failed me. Scampering squirrels and soaring birds did not elevate my mood. Finally, at the third mile, my breathing settled. My mood lightened.

I entered the Trail and ran north toward downtown New Freedom, where visitors were stepping up onto the black steam locomotive that would transport them for an hour or so through history. A train driver in blue-denim overalls and a matching brimmed engineer's cap stood in the cab. He pulled a cord, and the train's shrill whistle blasted. On a sidewalk, a middle-aged woman in a long prairie skirt, lacy white blouse, and black lace-up boots with a small heel as well as several men in 19th-century attire, black frock coats and checkered three-piece suits, milled around spouting snippets about past life in the town.

I needed a potty break. I ducked inside the women's restroom next to the Rail Trail Café. When I exited a few minutes later, three quarter horses—a bay, a black, and a chestnut—ridden by men in cowboy hats, western shirts, jeans, chaps, and scuffed leather boots with silver spurs stood near the bottom of the steps. The brown-haired ruddy-faced rider on the black horse's back leaned forward on its neck and stared quizzically at me. Perhaps, my sole brown face in a sea of pink faces piqued his puzzlement. I allowed my mind to wander. In an earlier time in US history, this man might have considered capturing me. My ancestors had been free long before the US Civil War, but my status as a free woman would not have necessarily saved me from being sold down the river. Being a free person had not saved the narrator of *Twelve Years a Slave* (1853). Then and now, people of African descent were perennially imperiled in the land of Uncle Sam.

As I was about to descend from the steps to the Trail, the bay horse backed up in my direction. Its rider, a white-bearded man resembling Gabby Hayes, an actor who appeared from the mid-1930s to the mid-1950s in numerous westerns as a bewhiskered old codger, beckoned toward me. "Come on down. You're all right. He'll stop," he said. I descended. I was not afraid of horses.

Decades earlier, I rode them for pleasure. I dabbled briefly with the notion of purchasing a Tennessee walking horse until sanity intervened.

After weaving my way through the visitors enthralled by the costumed women and men and by the riders, I ran north past a general store with huge pots of rose-mallow hibiscus plants, their red brightening the gray porch, and onward to the white-painted and red-shuttered Jackson House Bed and Breakfast in Railroad, where I U-turned. Clanking and hissing, the steam engine approached as I ran southward. I looked inside the compartments loaded with passengers. The train passed so close to me that I could see inside easily. I caught the eyes of an auburn-haired little girl. She smiled, and I waved to her. She waved in return.

I ran south for two more miles. Then a miracle happened. I rubbed my eyes. There Gracie stood. Her humans and she walked toward me. Smiling broadly, I stopped abruptly. I fawned, "This is the first time I've encountered Gracie when she wasn't on your lawn behind the electric fence." Good naturedly, her humans laughed.

"May I touch her?" I asked.

"Of course," they said in unison.

I caressed the wiry white, brown, and gray hair of her neck, her tummy, and her back. She rested her head on my hand and licked it. For the first time ever, she talked to me. She murmured, "I like you, too."

HORROR: CONFEDERATE FLAGS NEAR THE TRAIL

When I was a college student, I learned that the Confederate States of America (CSA) existed as an unrecognized country in North America from 1861 to 1865. Formed initially by seven slave-holding states (Alabama, Florida, Georgia, Louisiana, Mississippi, South Carolina, and Texas), the CSA was joined later by four other slave states (Arkansas, North Carolina, Tennessee, and Virginia). Subsequently, Missouri and Kentucky joined the Confederacy but never formally seceded from the United States.

The CSA adopted many flags, including three national ones—the Stars and Bars, the Stainless Banner, and the Blood-Stained Banner. The flag that I associated with the Confederacy was not one of these three, though. Instead, it was the Southern Cross, the battle flag of General Robert E. Lee's Army of Northern Virginia. It featured a blue diagonal cross, trimmed with white. White stars symbolizing the Confederate states were stitched inside the cross, which appeared against a red background. Involuntarily, I shuddered every single time I saw one of these symbols of hatred blowing in the wind or saw vehicle license plates or vehicle decals proclaiming allegiance to the CSA.

I could not elude such a flag when I ran south on the Trail. A quarter of a mile after I passed the Mason-Dixon Line, I looked through trees to my right and glimpsed a Southern Cross battle flag that interrupted the azure sky over a dingy white house speckled with green moss. A weedy lawn with three rusted-out cars on tire rims, a pickup truck on cinder blocks, a battered mahogany-colored pool table with ball-and-claw feet, and a dented gray-metal above-ground pool with slimy water spoke volumes.

The first time that I saw the flag, I was jarred and incensed. I never grew accustomed to it, but over time, it lost its impact. Or at least I thought that it did. I told myself that it was simply a part of the setting, a part that I loathed but could not change because the flag was located on private property.

I ran in this area approximately 100 times a year. I wondered whether the flag was a reason for the lack of racial diversity among visitors who walked, ran, and biked in this area. Only once had I seen a person of Asian descent, a woman who sat at one of the wooden picnic tables near the Mason-Dixon Line where bikers often congregated when they needed a break. Her royal-blue hybrid bike leaned against a tree. She waved and smiled broadly at me as she chewed slowly on something that she had taken from a bright-green insulated lunch bag. I remembered then that I had not eaten since early morning. I checked my watch. The time was 12:30 p.m. My stomach rumbled. Had she noticed the flag before she sat at the table? If she had, she might have thought that it did not pertain to her.

A few minutes later, when I ran farther south of the flag, I encountered a baby-faced African-American male who appeared to be in his early twenties. An exacta! Two non-Whites within 10 minutes. Heading north, he wore a black hydration vest on his back. I assumed that he had been running. As I passed him, he was slowly strolling and chatting on a cell phone. He must have happened upon one of the few spots in the area with fleeting connectivity. I had been shocked to see the Asian woman, but I was floored when he appeared. He grinned and pulled out his ear bud closer to me. "Hi," he said. I smiled back at him. Would he notice the flag on his left as he walked northward?

This particular Confederate flag was not my only encounter with this symbol of racial hostility on the Trail. Once when my schedule required that I cover 18 miles, I ran toward Glen Rock. This was my first foray so far north. Zoning out, I focused on my form. Then I was jolted. Over a street named Misty Meadows

Lane, which crossed the Trail, loomed a Stars and Bars Confederate flag with thick horizontal red and white lines and a blue square containing 13 stars (one for each state in the CSA) arranged in a circle. The flag was at least twice the size of the one near the Mason-Dixon sign. The mammoth flag near Misty Meadows Lane blew in the wind above a ramshackle gray house with a peeling-paint white porch. The yard was strewn with broken kitchen chairs and rusty automobile parts. Timeworn plastic sunflowers, their bright yellow dimmed by dust and dirt, rose haphazardly from the ground. I decided at that moment that I would never run so far in this direction again.

Although I thought that I had become desensitized to the Confederate flag near the Mason-Dixon Line, I learned that such was not so. One spring afternoon as I ran, I saw a family—a fit-looking bald man in blue-and-white plaid shorts that emphasized his taut gluteal muscles; a trim brunette woman whose panty line was visible under tan Capri pants; a blonde-haired girl, about nine years old, wearing a blush-pink top and matching Capri pants; and a blue-helmeted boy, about six years old, wearing gray shorts and pedaling a red and black bicycle. The girl grasped a leash attached to a black standard poodle's collar while the man held a leash controlling a cream standard poodle a little smaller than the black one. The group meandered to such an extent that I caught up with them and was indeed quite close to them when they passed the flag. The man looked startled and then uncomfortable. I saw no evidence that the children or the woman noticed it. At this point, I passed the group. My face warmed, and I felt strangely responsible for the flag's presence. The man smiled and said, "Hi." I responded, "Your dogs are beautiful." Actually, my descriptor applied only to the black one, but I did not want to exclude the other dog.

Shortly after I moved ahead of the family, a gray-brown cottontail hopped suddenly across my path. Once it was among some bushes, it sat stone still. I assumed that it thought it was unseen because it blended into the setting. The rabbit's round white tail betrayed it, of course. Spotting it easily, I focused on its huge brown eyes and became lost in their warm luminescence. My face cooled. Inside and outside, I felt heartened. I turned my head and looked backward in response to the laughter of the girl and boy who frolicked with the poodles in foot-deep Trail-side water that was more rapids than babbling brook.

A few months later, I finished a six-mile run on the Trail that ended near the spot where the boy and girl played with their dogs in the water. I had not run in the area recently. I decided to stroll home although, as probably one of the world's slowest walkers, I knew that covering a little more than a mile would take me at least 25 minutes. As I strode past the rundown property that was home to the Southern-Cross flag, I stopped short. Gone was this symbol of hatred and racism. A thirtyish man with long blonde hair, the first person I had ever seen on the property, was cutting down, gathering, and stacking tree limbs. Gone were the green spots on the house. The lawn had been mowed and cleared of discards. Instead of the pool table, there was a single rectangle, about six feet wide by 15 feet long, protected by a white tarpaulin. Through a gap in the covering, I saw green plants thriving. The above-ground pool, now free of slime and algae, contained clear water. A new day, perhaps.

A few weeks later when I ran past, a Stars and Bars flag, large and bright and new, waved.

Fear on the Trail: To Arm or Not to Arm

Sometimes, I ran miles and miles on the Trail without encountering anyone. During these runs, my mind drifted occasionally to news reports about rapes and murders of solo women runners. To stay out of harm's way as much as possible, I told David about the places where I planned to run, I ran while the sun shone, and I varied my departure-from-home times and my routes.

Additionally, I obtained defensive tools to deter human adversaries, devices that I usually forgot to tote. I bought a can of pepper spray containing three to six bursts. I purchased a wrist-fastened device with claws that I could use both to defend myself and to collect DNA. I ordered a ring with a serrated hump that I could use to make a jagged cut in a human attacker's flesh before he broke my finger or otherwise manhandled me.

When I pondered out loud about the wisdom of running with a gun, 99.9 percent of my running acquaintances responded in horror. Their reactions were not all that surprising. According to a 2016 survey published in *Runner's World*, only a small percentage of runners (two percent of men and one percent of women) reported that they sometimes carried guns. The fact that more men than women "packed heat" surprised me. Maybe more men were comfortable with firearms.

I had few reservations about guns. I had grown up with them. During the first 13 years of my life when my family lived in rural Maryland, a rifle regularly rested against one of our interior walls. My parents transported their guns, this same rifle and a revolver, to Baltimore when our family relocated there. In the city, my father owned a small convenience store. He bought a semiautomatic handgun and kept it on a shelf below the cash register. Sometimes he brought it home, where my sisters and I could have fingered it along with the rifle and the revolver had we so desired.

To ensure that I had some mastery of handguns, in 2015, I enrolled in a basic National Rifle Association handgun course offered by a Maryland gun club whose membership was approximately 95 percent African American and around 50 percent female, facts that surprised me. As passionate about their Second-Amendment Rights as a stereotypical right-wing survivalist group might be and pleased as punch about their extensive gun collections, the club members, at the beginning of the course, passed around their semi-automatic pistols and their revolvers so that we neophytes could gawk at and admire the weapons in hushed, worshipful tones. Under the group's tutelage, I shot paper targets in their paper hearts and aced the course.

In gun-friendly Pennsylvania, I could easily purchase a gun by completing an application at a gun shop or gun show and by undergoing a background check. If the gun remained inside my home, I would not need a license. To carry a gun outside the home, I would need to complete an "Application for a Pennsylvania License to Carry Firearms" in which I attested to being of good character and to being at least 21 years old. The application fee was $20. No training was required. The license would be in force for five years from the date that it was issued. The cost of renewal was also $20; no training was required.

Since I ran regularly into Maryland, I would want to be able to carry a gun there as well. A problem with this desire was that the state's handgun laws were much more restrictive than were Pennsylvania's. In addition to attesting to being an adult of good character, as a first-time applicant for a Maryland-gun license, I would be required to complete sixteen hours of firearms-safety training. The license would be in effect for three years.

Thereafter, the requirement would be eight hours of training for a renewal. The nonrefundable cost of the initial application was $75, and the renewal cost was $50.

I thought long and hard about what I should do. Seek gun-carry licenses in both states? Or in Pennsylvania only? Or in neither state? Then one Sunday afternoon, I ran in a Maryland section of the Trail where few people biked, ran, or walked. As I bustled along at about 10:00 pace, a male walker set off alarms throughout my body: his listing-ship walk, his sallow skin, his slack-jawed and pock-marked face, his slicked-down dirty-blonde hair, and his dark-brown leather jacket from glory days long past. His physical appearance and aura evoked photographs of Richard Speck, killer of eight student nurses in Chicago in 1966, three years after I graduated from high school. When I ran by the man on my way south, I calmly said, "Hi." Greeting him was intended as a message that he did not frighten me although he did. Conventional wisdom was that if a person seemed confident and strong, a prospective wrongdoer might be less likely to harm her. As an addition to my no-fear message, I summoned every shred of my speed and aggression and left him in my wake. After three more miles, I U-turned and ran north, hoping that he had abandoned the Trail.

"Oh, God! No!" Slowly, he moved toward me. What would I do if he yanked me off the Trail and did Lord knows what to me? As I panicked, a biker came up behind me and passed me on my left. I had not heard his churning wheels. Startled, I masked my fear and calmly said "Hello" to the biker.

The walking man moved closer and closer toward me. With my hands clenched into fists, I sped up and ran straight at him, emphasizing, I hoped, that if he messed with me, he would have a fight on his hands. I also ran fast because I wanted to be beyond his arm's reach while the biker was still within earshot. I did not speak to the walker as I darted by him. One greeting per person during a single run was my rule on the Trail no matter how many times I encountered him or her. I ran and ran until I could no longer see him when I peeked over my shoulder.

When I told David about the walking man, he chuckled and said, "He probably wondered why this crazy little woman was barreling directly toward him."

Shortly thereafter, I learned that Maryland gun-carry permits were granted only to applicants who demonstrated that wearing or transporting handguns was necessary as a precaution against danger. I doubted that my fear of being attacked while running was a sufficient reason. When I ran into Maryland, I would have to decide whether I would illegally carry a lightweight handgun inside a holster or inside a zippered pocket of my running tights or shorts or whether I would hide a two-shot derringer in my running bra. Being charged with a violation of handgun laws would be small potatoes compared to being a victim of an assault.

Eventually, I bought a Ruger LCP, a compact and powerful weapon, and I obtained a Pennsylvania gun-carry license. But the gun did not join me on my runs. I limited myself to the streets of New Freedom, where usually as the only African-American woman runner around, I was extremely visible for better or worse. I continued to run on sections of the Trail with heavy foot traffic and avoided runs into the area where I had seen the man resembling Richard Speck.

RUNNING WOES: TINKLING, NAUSEA, AND TROTS

During my runs, the same woes surfaced again and again. Since they could easily blow up my runs, I named them TNT (an acronym for tinkling, nausea, and trots).

From the start of my running days, the urgent need to tinkle plagued me. I attributed my whizzing urges to heredity—to Mama. Decades earlier whenever my mother, my sisters, and I traveled slightly more than 100 miles north by car from our longtime home in St. Mary's County to Baltimore, Mama drove the car off the road at least twice each way because she had to tinkle. She blamed these stops on a weak bladder caused by seven vaginal childbirths. Six of us survived, but one of our siblings, a boy, passed away during infancy. She mourned him until the day she died.

Curious, my sisters and I bunched together on the back seat of the car and rose on our knees whenever the car stopped for this reason. We peered out the dusty rear window as Mama tiptoed along road shoulders on trash-strewn sections of US 301 and squatted tentatively behind thick bushes or a tree. Daddy did not accompany us on any of these trips. My parents were probably estranged yet again.

With Mama's role modeling, during training runs, I was never reluctant to relieve myself by finding a spot in a bend of a road or by taking advantage of a path with a recessed one-adult wide space where trees or bushes hid me from view. When I wore a running skirt in warm weather, after ensuring that no one was in view, I pulled the shorts under the skirt to the side and leaned forward a tad. When cold weather dictated that I wear capris or long pants, I dropped them halfway down my thighs after surveilling the area and squatted. This approach worked well when the Trail or some other wooded area was passable. When snow limited my runs to asphalt streets lined with houses and businesses, I urinated on myself. To decrease the prospective stench in my shoes, when I reached home on such days, I sprayed them with a bacteria-busting mist or showered them with so much odor-reducing powder that they seemed to be trapped in a permanent winter. After years of tinkling on myself during winters, I discovered female urination devices (FUDs)—funnels popular with women who hike and climb. According to David, the devices were called "she urinals"; they allowed women to urinate standing up like men. I bought one in soft silicone. It was so small that I carried it in a pocket in my running pants, in a jacket pocket, or in a water-vest pocket.

During races, when I needed to tinkle, I kept going. I did not even slow down as warm urine crept down my legs. To ensure that onlookers did not realize what I had done, like many other runners with a similar problem, I wore black running bottoms. Moisture is barely visible on fabric of this color. If I waited for awards ceremonies and had sufficient time, I found a safe spot, often with David standing guard, where I changed into a clean skirt, shorts, or pants that I had stowed in his car. If I had no time to change, I dried my clothing and body as much as I could with napkins or paper towels that I picked up from refreshment areas, plastered a smile on my face, and pretended that all was right with the world.

Over time, I learned that I was hardly unique with respect to tinkling. Many women, largely those over 50 years of age, leaked or full out urinated on themselves during high-impact activities. (Male runners rarely suffered from this problem because of their anatomy; they have longer urethra and a double ring of muscle to squeeze off the bladder and urethra.) Causes of women's incontinence included pelvic weakness because of hormonal changes, pregnancy, and childbirth as well as gravity's weakening and stretching of the pelvic region as time marched on.

To prevent tinkling, women resorted to several techniques. If a weak bladder was the suspected cause, they inserted tampons or tampon-like products into the vagina to support the bladder. When I tried this approach, insertion was fairly easy, but removing the tampon took ten agonizing minutes. (Maybe I should have used a lubricant.) This effort was in vain, for I urinated as often as I had in the past.

After many years with this problem, I met with Anne, a physical therapist who specialized in women's pelvic issues. She told me that incontinence was a problem for approximately 40 percent of women runners. As she talked, I began to understand that, unlike Mama's weakened pelvic-floor muscles, mine were constantly contracted. During runs, my pelvic-floor muscles were tightened for prolonged periods as they held in place my intestines, vagina, uterus, bladder, urethra, and rectum. Constant contraction led to a frequent urge to urinate. During physical therapy, I learned how to relax my pelvic muscles. To achieve this end, I was required to perform reverse kegels (releasing the muscles while standing, sitting, or lying down with the knees bent) and to use a vaginal dilator (a hard plastic device one-quarter of an inch in diameter and six inches long in my case) that I lubricated and inserted. The dilator functioned as a foam roller of sorts and eliminated pelvic-muscle knots. Additionally, during visits, Anne placed surgical gloves on her hands and manually relaxed my pelvic muscles.

She recommended that I train my body so that I could run two to three hours without tinkling, the standard for most people. The process would be a gradual one. She told me that before running, I should sip rather than gulp room-temperature water. A benefit of sipping would be improved hydration. If I drank slowly, my body should absorb the liquid more fully than if I consumed it quickly. I should wait at least two hours after I drank before I ran. I should cease drinking pre-run coffee, a diuretic. Unable to follow this last recommendation fully, I compromised by cutting the ounces in half. When I ran, if I felt the urge to tinkle, I had to postpone stopping. One of the most effective ways to do this was through distraction.

In some instances, runners refocused their thoughts by singing along with music or playing games in their heads. I adopted the latter. I played *Spellbound*, a word game to which I was addicted. Running, I could not play the game exactly as I did on my computer. Online, the word game provided a random assortment of letters from which the player forms words during a two-minute period. Because I could not remember a string of random letters as I ran and because I had little sense of how much time passed as I formed words, I began with a word that I could easily remember. Then I came up with as many words of three or more letters as I could. I imposed no time limit on myself. For some reason, the word "gibberish," a particularly appropriate choice, was the first one that I thought of when I began to play this game. With no time constraint, I came up with words such as "bribes," "heirs," and "ergs" easily.

Nausea was another woe that negatively affected my running. Years would pass before I learned the cause of my problem. Every time a wave of queasiness hit me, I walked until it passed. I talked with other runners about this problem. One of them speculated that dehydration might be the cause. She told me that, to prevent this condition, she drank a specific amount of water that was a function of her body weight. She weighed 110 pounds and drank at least 67 or so ounces of water daily, half her weight in ounces of water plus 10 to 15 percent of her weight. I weighed 120 pounds most of the time. Using this model, I began to drink approximately 70 ounces of water every day. To achieve this objective, I slowly sipped 8 ounces of water after I got out of bed each morning. Depending on the weather and distance, I drank from 8 to 16 ounces when I ran. After my run, I poured a fizzy multi-vitamin powder into 16 ounces of water and drank the brew. I consumed at least 12 ounces of water with my post-run meal and slurped at least 12 ounces of water with dinner. To meet my quota, I lugged around a thermal water bottle and drank the rest of my daily water requirement from it throughout the day. No doubt, as I sucked from the bottle's nipple, I resembled an over-age toddler.

When this approach failed to prevent nausea, I asked my primary-care physician to recommend a remedy. She suggested 75 milligrams of Zantac to reduce stomach acids that build up overnight and cause motion-induced nausea. Dutifully, for months, I swallowed Zantac every morning before I ran. At first, the drug forestalled nausea. Then it did not prevent or delay it. Thus, I stopped taking it. (Years later, the medication was withdrawn from the US market because of negative side effects.)

Serendipitously, I found a resolution to the problem. One night during dinner with friends, I mentioned my nausea. A physician in the group suggested that I eat something prior to running to deal with the stomach acids that formed overnight. Through trial and error, I settled on a quarter of a cranberry-nut bagel before a run up to six miles, a half bagel before runs up to 12 miles or so, and a whole bagel before runs up to 20 miles. I ate two hours before I ran. My nausea was no more.

As a destroyer of runs, trots (or pooping or pooing) was the most daunting of the three woes. Trots, an uncontrollable urge to defecate, seemed to be a taboo topic even among runners who routinely removed their socks to display black and blue toenails, who described vomit in exhaustive detail, who pulled up their shorts to show their rubbed-raw thighs, and who publicly popped bulbous foot blisters.

Trots occurred as a result of the jarring of the stomach during running. Runners across a broad spectrum of abilities have been bedeviled by this problem. A famous photograph of "poopy" Uta

Pippig winning the 1996 Boston Marathon women's race with watery feces (and menstrual blood) dripping down her legs probably haunts many a female racer. In a much-distributed photograph nine years after Pippig's trots episode, another world-class woman runner, Paula Radcliffe, was captured on film as she squatted on the 2005 London-Marathon course to relieve herself. She called her decision to defecate 22 miles into the race "an embarrassing necessity." She was focused on winning and knew stomach cramps were slowing her. To run as fast as possible, she explained, she needed "to go." She won her third London Marathon that day in world-record time.

During the 2011 Boston Marathon, I understood how Pippig and Radcliffe felt when I needed to poop in the worst way. I had made the rookie error of eating a pre-race meal, oatmeal, which I had not tested prior to the race. Around mile 16, I could no longer beat back the urge. Finding an empty porta-potty on the course was easy. What was difficult was untying my running skirt's drawstring, which I had knotted tightly multiple times. After what seemed like a century and hundreds of attempts to loosen my skirt, I contracted my buttocks as tightly as possible and managed to inch my skirt down. I have no idea how much actual time I lost before I resumed the marathon.

From that point forward, I feared trots. Too many times, my body forced me to hop behind a tree in Druid Hill Park and once behind a business sign on a traffic-heavy city street when I did not have enough control, and thus not enough time, to reach a runner-friendly coffee shop or supermarket.

I became so poop obsessed that I began to think occasionally of myself not as a person but instead as a crustacean whose existence was defined by the black line running from its mouth to its anus. Called a sand vein or a poop shute, this line is the intestinal tract, a tube filled with excrement and the remains of whatever the creature has eaten. Many times, I had removed this tract from shrimp and lobsters as I prepared to cook them.

Minimizing the likelihood of trots became a mission. Before training runs, I fine-tuned my nightly eating schedule so that I could promptly empty my sand vein in the morning and be ready to run two hours after I awakened. I ate dinners chocked full of high-fiber carbohydrates such as skin-on potatoes, broccoli, and Brussel sprouts as well as small amounts of animal protein promptly at 5:30 p.m. Most nights I ate five or six pitted fiber-rich prunes for dessert.

When I had a race, my dinners consisted largely of carbohydrates but with a difference. I consumed a whopping serving of rotini pasta with tomato sauce that included oodles of pitted briny kalamata olives and a small serving of grilled shrimp two nights before the race and a smaller serving of the same meal the night before the race. I needed the extra carbs and the salt. Prunes were verboten 24 hours before a race; they might come back to haunt me. I awakened four hours before the start time. I gulped a small amount of coffee to stimulate the emptying of my bowels.

In *Marathon*, Saint Hal revealed that he jogged on a hotel parking lot to get things going when he traveled for a race. When I was away from home, I emulated him to some degree; however, as a woman, I did not feel safe trotting alone on a parking lot in the early morn. When the hotel had a treadmill in its fitness room, I ran on it to jostle my body. If no treadmill was available, I ran in place in my room. At home when I trained, I never considered venturing outside to jar my innards. I feared that my neighbors might see me running around on my dew-covered lawn in a pink teddy and diagnose my behavior as lunacy and report me to the homeowners' association as a menace to propriety. Instead, I bounced down to my basement, hopped on my treadmill, and slowly jogged until I felt the urge.

Battling Insomnia and Rarely Winning

A common assumption is that physical exercise improves the ability to sleep well. But such is not true for many runners and other endurance athletes. Several of the women in the Druid-Hill-Park running group slept poorly as did Margaret, my long-time running partner. Some researchers believe that insomnia among such people is often tied to the personality characteristics of those who are attracted to running—competitive, driven, and disciplined individuals who push themselves, often relentlessly.

My mind wandered as Dr. Ekaterina Howland chatted with me yet again about my insomnia. For two years, from 2015 to 2017, I met with her. A caring and patient medical doctor specializing in integrative health, she was an African-American woman in her early forties who had earned a bachelor's degree with honors in chemistry from Amherst College and a medical degree from Columbia University College of Physicians and Surgeons. Dr. Howland and I agreed, from the beginning of our sessions, that my objective was to reduce first and eliminate later my dependence on Ambien, which I had taken in increasing dosages since 1998, when I was diagnosed with breast cancer and needed something to help me to sleep. My dosage when I began to meet with Dr. Howland was 10 milligrams nightly, a mega dose for a woman of my size.

I had been spacing out when she grabbed my attention by saying, "Athletes need sleep." I resisted the temptation to look around the room to see whether someone else might be present.

"Me, an athlete?"

"Yes, you."

After this brief exchange, she encouraged me to return to nightly breathing exercises that she had demonstrated in the past. I should inhale for four seconds and slowly exhale for eight seconds. She urged me to return to progressive muscle relaxation—another approach she had recommended in earlier sessions. She reminded me of how I should tense and then relax muscle groups. Neither the breathing exercises nor the relaxation techniques had helped me to get to sleep in the past. They had led only to frustration and wakefulness. Despite their ineffectiveness, I agreed to try them again.

Dr. Howland reminded me that I should flip a switch when I went to bed. I should practice mindfulness, anchoring myself in the present and avoiding thoughts about the past and the future. Also, she encouraged me to focus on calming thoughts. In the past, I had chosen to think about chipmunks and squirrels, creatures that I encountered often during my runs. Rarely did my calming thoughts revolve around people—except for a seven-year-old neighbor boy I claimed, with his mother's permission, as a surrogate grandson. Unable to be at home one December afternoon when he hopped off his yellow school bus, she asked me to meet him and take him to my house. Although the stop was only about 400 feet from my front door, I drove to pick him up because the temperature was in the low 30s. Immediately after he jumped off the bus, he whined, "I want to go to my own house." I explained that I did not have the key. For a reason that I never learned, he was dressed that day like a mini businessman. As soon as we entered my house, he dropped his tan trench coat on the floor of the family room, removed his little leather belt and his clip-on tie and let them fall near his coat, untucked his white dress shirt, plopped himself onto the sofa facing the 62-inch television screen, and wriggled his feet out of his brown wing-tip shoes. On the coffee table, I placed a glass of icy-cold milk and freshly baked, still-warm, dark-chocolate cookies studded with dark-chocolate chunks. I turned on *Sponge Bob Square Pants*. He nestled into the sofa, smiled, and said, "I feel like Santa Claus." At first, I did not understand what he meant. Then I remembered that Christmas was a week or so away. Five hours later when I went to bed, I had a dream during which I laughed, a never-before and never-after experience.

During one of our sessions, Dr. Howland suggested a major cause of my insomnia. "You're suffering from imposter syndrome. Deep down, you doubt yourself. You're a perfectionist. You'll do almost anything to achieve at the highest level," she said quietly. "If you don't reach this standard, your negative feelings about yourself increase." She thought that if I could learn to see myself differently, I might reduce my anxiety and might sleep more easily. Gently, she added, "This self-training isn't going to happen overnight. With help and constant reinforcement, you're going to be able to believe that you're a worthy person." I nodded my head in agreement although I did not believe that I could do as she suggested.

She smiled. "What happens is that you're constantly caught up in a vicious cycle. You're happy with yourself for a little while shortly after you receive some token of your value. Like a sieve, you feel empty quickly, though. You need something else to make you feel good about yourself. When you were working, you pursued another project. I'm sure you put in outrageous hours and you set the highest standards for yourself and for others. Probably, you were labeled a workaholic."

She added, "If you're honest with yourself, you'd admit that you worked so hard for all those hours because you were addicted to the validation that success brought." She continued, "Now as a runner, you sign up for another race." I nodded in agreement.

While I saw Dr. Howland, over time I decreased my Ambien dosage and then totally stopped taking the medication. Then some occurrence, so inconsequential that I could not remember what it was, slipped into bed with me one night and penetrated my thoughts to such an extent that I sought refuge in Ambien again.

Shortly thereafter, Dr. Howland left Maryland for a position in Michigan, and no integrative-medicine physician replaced her. Seeking still to end my dependence on Ambien, I made an appointment at a sleep-disorders center, where I met every two weeks for several months with Dr. Juan Santiago, a cognitive-behavioral psychologist. Initially, he asked that I wear a sleep monitor at home for two nights, and based on the results, he and I set up a schedule that barred electronics after 9:00 p.m. but permitted television as long as I was at least six feet away from the screen. When I watched television between 10:00 p.m. and 11:00 p.m., I limited my viewing to innocuous shows focusing on house hunting, cooking competitions, and house flipping. The episodes of these shows were so indistinguishable from one another that I could not remember later which episodes I had seen and which ones I had not.

Dr. Santiago recommended other strategies. He told me to stop drinking liquids at 9:00 p.m.; thus, I was less likely to have to get up at night for bathroom trips. He suggested that I push plugs into my ear canals each night so that David's light snoring did not keep me awake. He allowed me to take 5 milligrams of Ambien an hour before bedtime initially; he hoped that eventually I would cut the dosage in half gradually and then eliminate the drug totally. We agreed that I should be in bed by 11:00 p.m. and I should arise by 7:00 a.m. or thereabouts.

Additionally, Dr. Santiago believed that reframing my thoughts, seeing an incident or episode or people through a different and more positive lens, was a key step toward beating back the thoughts that caused my mind to race when I was in bed. I tried to implement this approach, but it did not lead to a lack of dependence on Ambien. I continued to gulp five-milligram tablets nightly. Now and then I robbed Peter to pay Paul. When taking 5 milligrams did not lead to sleep, I bit off a chunk of a second tablet. When I was totally out of Ambien because of taking too much during the 30-day prescription period, I resorted to over-the-counter sleep aids that left me groggy for hours after I awakened.

Metamorphosis came slowly because my self-worth had been inextricably tied to external acknowledgments of my value throughout my entire life—so much so that just before I earned my bachelor's degree, nightmares about graduating as the salutatorian instead of the valedictorian haunted me night after night. Being second was the same as losing. After I graduated first in my class, nightmares revolving around my academic performance still haunted me. In these dreams, I was again a student striving for a bachelor's degree, and I was enrolled in a biochemistry course and an organic-chemistry course for which I had neither preparation nor predilection. In my nightmares, I earned F grades in these courses, and I browbeat the registrar into removing the courses and grades from my transcript. More often, nightmares about my termination from one professional position after another recurred.

Ridding myself of these nightmares should have been motivation enough to remove Ambien from my nighttime ritual. In 2018, 20 years after I began to take the drug off and on but usually on, I read an article that revealed that people who took Ambien were more likely to recall negative or upsetting memories. Unwittingly, for decades, I had resurrected self-doubts most nights. Unfortunately, this knowledge did not lead to my total abandonment of Ambien. But it did lead to a reduction of the amount that I took each night. Usually, I was able to sleep after biting off a little more than half of a chunk (about 3 milligrams) of a 5-milligram tablet.

DEBACLE: THE 2016 BOSTON MARATHON (MY SEVENTH MARATHON)

Cascading calamities. The Fates scowled at me on April 18, 2016, the date of the 120th Boston Marathon. Had I honored their signs, I would have rushed to one of the buses that traveled back and forth between Boston and Hopkinton, returned to Boston, and lain around all day at the Boston Marriott Hotel second guessing my decision not to run in the marathon.

The first omen. The band separated from the face of my GPS watch. Clatter! All the pieces fell to the ground as I stood chatting with a stranger in the slowest, and last, group of runners. The pin that held the band in place skipped across the asphalt. I bent over and picked up the pieces, but I could not put the watch together again. Reattachment of the components required a special tool.

David's GPS watch was on top of the dresser in my hotel room. I had brought it with me to Boston as a backup, but I did not wear it on the day of the race. Superstitious, I told myself that I needed to wear the exact same watch that I had worn in every single race prior to this one. Had I possessed the gift of foresight, I would have worn both watches.

The second harbinger. The day before I flew to Boston, I learned that the Boston Athletic Association prohibited runners from wearing hydration vests on their backs. This ban was tied to the 2013 bombings; the Tsarnaev brothers transported their bombs in backpacks. Hydration vests looked like backpacks. So the logic (or illogic) went.

Like legendary marathoner Bill Rodgers, I found drinking water from a cup or a bottle while running challenging. Indeed, to the amazement of onlookers, he came to a full stop to drink water during the 1975 Boston Marathon, which he won. He explained, "It is always tricky getting your water, so I just came to a complete halt and would drink it." He added, "I think that worked. I didn't stop long. I took a few gulps and then I was gone." To drink from a cup, I, too, had to stop.

With a water vest, I could both drink and run simultaneously. All I had to do was grab the tube hanging from the bladder, enclosed in a compartment on my back, and bite down on the valve through which water flowed. Such easy access to fluids was more than worth the additional weight on my back, weight that would diminish as I drank more and more water.

At the eleventh hour, I drove to a running store and experimented with hydration methods. I tried a belt that fit around my waist and that accommodated small bottles of water, the only liquid that I could drink when I was running. I could not easily balance the belt on my hips. I removed it from consideration.

I already owned a belt with a holder for a large bottle on my lower back. I had worn it only once. I just could not tolerate its thumping against my vertebrae. Also, I disliked having to twist my body or reach behind to grab the bottle from my lower back. It joined a pile of castoff fitness items on my kitchen-pantry floor.

Finally, I settled on a hand-held bottle with a sturdy soft-fabric case that I already owned. After inserting a rubber straw into the opening at the top of the bottle, I could drink easily while running. No need to hold up the bottle and tilt my head upward and cough or choke as a few drops of water trickled between my lips. I was good to go.

The best-laid plans. When my GPS watch fell apart, I patted myself on the back because I came up with a solution quickly, or so I thought. I used safety pins to attach the watch face to the cloth case around the water bottle. My having pins with me was a stroke of good fortune. Or so I thought. I had never carried them in the past, but for this race, I wanted to be prepared for every eventuality.

A major problem. I forgot gravity. Every time I checked the pace on my pinned-on watch, the water leaked through the straw as I raised and lowered the bottle.

The temperature at Hopkinton was around 70 degrees, much hotter than in 2011 when I ran the Boston Marathon for the first time. (The 2016 version of the marathon was the fourth hottest race start since 2000.) In southern Pennsylvania, I had been training in 40- to 50-degree weather. Acclimatizing generally takes two weeks. I had only one day.

I ran fairly well until I neared mile 18. At this point, I sought help in a medical tent, where I was asked to lie down as soon as I stumbled in. As I lay there on a rigid cot, a tall brown-haired woman with a stethoscope circling her neck rushed over. I looked at the badge that she was wearing. It read Physician Assistant Joan Finch. I had assumed she was a nurse. Gender bias?

"Do you know your name?" she asked in a clipped professional manner.

I answered, "Yes. T. J. Bryan."

"How do you feel?"

"Dizzy. Weak."

"How long have you felt like this?"

"For about five minutes or so before I stopped here."

I shivered. Glistening goose bumps on my forearms felt like tiny wet stones.

"Any other symptoms?"

"I felt such painful side stitches that I could barely walk to the tent."

"What did you do?

"I held my breath."

"You should have inhaled deeply and slowly. Also, you should have pressed the stitch."

"So I did exactly the wrong thing."

"How often had you been drinking water?"

"I tried to drink water at each stop after I had run ten miles, but the tiny cups were only half full."

"You should have started drinking as soon as you began the race and then at least every two miles."

She continued her lecture.

"You're an experienced marathoner, aren't you? You must've run in at least one other marathon."

Strange statement. She must have known about runners who earned entries because of their fundraising and not became of their past participation in marathons.

I answered, "Yes on both counts."

"You didn't learn in your earlier races that you shouldn't wait until you're thirsty to start drinking?"

"I always wore a water vest on my back during races. I didn't know until the last minute that the Boston Athletic Association banned such vests."

Then I exploded as much as I could in my weakened state. I exclaimed, "I don't understand why they're banned! No runner with a water vest caused the bombings!"

She ignored my rant.

"Did you consume energy gel or drink Gatorade during the run?"

"I can't stomach Gatorade."

"Gels?"

"No, not really. I need to drink a lot of water with gels, or else I become nauseous. When I finally stopped at a water stop, there was so little water in the cup that I postponed taking a gel."

"What did you consume before the race began?"

"Zantac."

The physician assistant's eyes seemed to pop out of their sockets like a cartoon character's might. Looking shocked, she asked, "Xanax?"

"No. Zantac! In the past, I used to be nauseous when I started running, and I took Zantac to deal with the problem. Later I learned that eating something small before running prevents queasiness. Although I stopped taking Zantac a while back, this morning I decided to take one as additional insurance."

Anything else?

"Emergen-C."

"You had an emergency this morning? What kind?"

"No, the vitamin-C and multi-vitamin powder."

"Did you eat any food this morning?"

"A few pretzels and a Clif Shots Espresso gel about three hours before the start of my wave."

"You do know that you should have eaten something more than that. Maybe a bagel with peanut butter and jelly. A banana and some white rice, perhaps."

"The last time I ran Boston, I ate some oatmeal. I got the trots, so I was afraid to eat anything much this time."

She turned toward a young man who looked like a college student. She said to him, "I'm going to take her vitals. I need you to write the numbers down for me."

She redirected her attention to me. She asked, "Who's your emergency contact?"

"My husband. Look at my shoe. His phone number is etched on my Road ID."

The young man chirped as he looked at my shoe. "What a great idea!"

I mumbled, "Wearing a shoe or bracelet ID is pretty common among runners and bikers. That way when someone finds you unconscious or dead on a road, your remains can be identified." I managed a weak smile.

He said, "This tag says you were born in 1945."

"True," I responded.

Looking shocked, he asked, "You're 70 years old?"

"Yes. I'll be 71 in a few months."

Meanwhile, the physician assistant pulled her cell phone from the deep recesses of her pants pocket. After peeping at my shoe, she typed in David's number. I heard the dull ringing of his phone before he answered. As soon as he said "Hello," she replied, "Your wife is in a medical tent on the Boston-Marathon course."

Her phone was in speaker mode. From David, silence followed.

Pushing myself up on my elbows, I reached for her phone and said, "I'll talk to him."

"Surprise," I said to him.

David was driving, he explained, and had not signed into runner tracking on the marathon website. He assumed that I would run well—as I had in every marathon up to that time. This race was hardly the first one to which I had traveled alone. In the past, not only had I run races without knowing a soul, but also I had driven alone to hosting cities that I had never visited prior to the races. After my conversation with David, the physician assistant told me that I had to lie back again. She warned, "You're going to be here for a while. I'm going to have to administer IV rehydration."

Her statement evoked memories of passages that I had read about legendary long-distance runner Alberto Salazar, nicknamed the "Mule" during his college years because of his tenacity. His mental toughness or perhaps near insanity propelled him to victories in three successive New York City Marathons (1980, 1981, and 1982). Determined to come in first in the 1982 Boston Marathon, he did not waste time drinking water during the race. He pushed, pushed, pushed. After winning the race, he was so dehydrated that he collapsed and required six liters of saline intravenously. This behavior was not unusual for him. Four years earlier, in 1978, the "Mule" ran so ferociously in the seven-mile Falmouth Road Race that he collapsed with a 107-degree temperature and a priest administered last rites. Salazar finished tenth.

I snapped out of my thoughts about Salazar when the physician assistant tapped my arm.

She said, "We're planning to send you to the finish in one of our vans."

I responded loudly, "I'm not getting on any 'SAG wag.'"

I continued, "If I can walk, I'm going to finish this race. I didn't come all this way and spend a lot of money for nothing. I need my finisher's medal."

The physician assistant purred, "Try to rest."

Seriously? My mind wandered as I lay there staring at the needle in a vein on the inside of my right arm. The clock was ticking. Finally, she gently removed the metal tip. After staunching the bleeding with a tiny cotton ball, she covered the area with another ball and taped it to my flesh. "You can stand up now," she said. I hopped up quickly and had to sit down on the side of the cot. I was unsteady.

She said, "Get up slowly this time. Hold onto me when you stand." I followed her instructions. After a few minutes had passed, I staggered out of the tent. As I began to run toward mile 19, her words trailed after me. "If you feel faint again, stop at the next tent." Loudly, I responded, I hoped convincingly. "You have my word. I will." If she believed me, she was one of the most gullible people on the planet. I would stop only after I crossed the finish line.

Running slowly into the cool Boston-area breeze, I shivered. My hands felt like chunks of ice. I still had close to seven miles to go.

When I lumbered across the finish line, the huge digital numbers read "6:00." I had begun 15 minutes after the first wave of non-elite runners. I had been on the course for almost five hours and 45 minutes once that 15-minute period was subtracted.

As soon as I entered my hotel room, I clicked on the Boston Athletic Association's website and found my times at specific junctures of the race. I ran the first 3.1 miles at 10:00 pace, a little faster than I had planned. I ran the second 3.1 miles in a little over 10:00 pace. I reached the half-marathon point in 2:14:19 and crossed the mat at 15.5 miles 26 minutes later in 2:40:54. Running fewer than four more miles consumed almost 45 minutes. Eighty minutes later, after spending what seemed like an eternity in the medical tent, I covered three more miles. I walked and ran the final 3.1 miles—a mixed approach that consumed 43 minutes. I finished almost dead last in my age group; I was 24 of 27 women in the 70-74 division. My final marathon time was 5:41:39. My pace was 13:02. Utter humiliation!!! I wondered then and later whether I should have taken a DNF (Did Not Finish).

People who knew my running abilities were shocked. Margaret assumed that I would run well and qualify for the 2017 Boston Marathon. She told me, "I checked once to see how you were doing. You were running early on around 10:00 pace as you had planned, so I stopped tracking you."

I confessed to Margaret, "I'm so ashamed." She consoled me: "You're an excellent runner who just had an off day. Don't put so much pressure on yourself. Think of the millions of people who never run a marathon."

She added, "Anyone who has raced more than one marathon knows anything can happen. I've had good marathon times and lousy ones. I'm proud of each and every one because I gave my best on that given day." I sighed. Her commonsense words did not comfort me. My best was not good enough.

Naively, I had deluded myself into believing that I would qualify for the Boston Marathon every single time that I ran a marathon although few runners achieved such consistency. After the 2016 Boston Marathon, I was forced, yet again, to accept that running was like other aspects of life. Preparation could be undone by circumstances that could not be controlled as well as by errors of judgment or lack of information. The parallels between my response to my professional end and my reaction to this marathon outcome did not escape me.

I attempted to make myself feel better about my performance by running in two 5Ks in quick succession. One occurred 22 days after the marathon. That some other 70-to-74-year-old woman might beat me to the finish line and grab the coveted first-place age-group award never occurred to me.

At the 5K, David muttered, "You shouldn't be racing today. You needed to take it easy for 26 days, one day for each mile you raced."

"I'm off by only four days."

"Considering your age, you probably need more time to rest."

"What!" I responded.

As I trotted to the line, I chatted with Cynthia, a pretty African-American woman who was about ten years younger than I was. I had met her a few years earlier at a local 5K when she won an age-group award. Curious about her racing past, on the same day that I met her, I checked her racing history on *Athlinks*, an online data bank that listed athletic-events results. There I learned that she had been competing for at least 15 years, that she raced almost every weekend from spring to early fall, and that she was a good regional 5K, 10K, half-marathon, and marathon runner. As time went by, Cynthia and I trained together occasionally and encountered one another often at Baltimore-area races.

That day Cynthia placed first in the 60-to-64 women's group, and I was first in the 70-99 women's group. The overall winner was Heather, a woman in her 30s who was an elite runner who had participated in the 2016 US Olympic Marathon Trials. Waiting for the awards ceremony, Heather and I chatted about nothing in particular at first, and then the topic drifted to weather conditions during the Trials. She said, "It was so hot in Los Angeles that many of the women dropped out. I made it through, but I finished midpack." Then I told her about my experience at the Boston Marathon. She said that she would have stopped running had she been in my place. "Elite runners DNF," she stated, "whenever they fear that continuing might result in injury." She added, "They don't think twice about stepping off a course under such circumstances."

A month later, I encountered Heather again when both of us ran in another 5K on the same course on which we had met.

Again, she was the overall winner, and I came in first in my age group. While I was pleased to see her a second time, this race was notable to me for another reason. When I picked up my award, something bizarre occurred. I was handed the second-place award. When I pointed this error out to the person presenting the awards, she was puzzled. Immediately, she made an announcement: "If someone picked up the 70-99 first-place women's award, can you please bring it back to the podium?" Sheepishly, a woman slowly came up and returned the award. A younger woman accompanied her. The two women came over to me later and told that the older woman had come in second. By a bunch! My time was 30:21, and my pace was 9:46. Her time was 58:22, and her pace was 18:46. The older woman was visiting the area and was accustomed, the younger woman explained, to finishing first in her age group. Really? I tried to resist the thought, but I guessed that had the younger woman not forced the return of the award, the older woman would have absconded with it. And I thought that I had issues. I was a piker in comparison.

Shortly after this 5K, my 2016 Boston-Marathon completion certificate appeared in the mailbox. I glared at it, ripped it into shreds, and tossed the pieces into the recycling bin. The only remaining pieces of evidence of my participation in the 2016 Boston Marathon were my finisher's medal, a long-sleeved royal-blue-and-yellow running shirt, and a blackish-blue nail on the big toe of my right foot. After loosening for months, the nail remained attached by the slimmest thread. Then one morning when I awoke, it was gone without a trace. I searched under the sheets, on the floor, and in every other nook and cranny in the bedroom. Perhaps the nail fairy had spirited it away.

Starstruck: Encounters with Running Superstars

A few months after the 2016 Boston Marathon, David and I flew five hours from the Baltimore-Washington International Airport to the Portland, Oregon, airport and rented a car that he drove to Eugene, Oregon, where the US Olympic Trials occurred at Historic Hayward Field on the University of Oregon campus. From July 1 through July 10, 2016, world-class athletes competed on or near the reddish track. On the green infield, they tossed javelins, threw hammers, vaulted over bars, and jumped into sandy pits. On the oval itself, athletes ran, they leaped over hurdles, or they leaped over water jumps.

When we purchased our tickets, we did not realize that we would be "riding" metal bleachers without cover from sun and rain. On the first day, our backs throbbed, and our derrieres became numb. That evening we rushed to a local Walmart to buy cushioned stadium seats with back support. The next few days we fried in the sun although we wore hats. To protect ourselves, we smeared so much sunscreen on our necks and arms that we looked like ghosts. Slathering on more white liquid than did David, I was motivated by a friend's frequent reminder, "Just because you have that brown skin doesn't mean you can't get sunburn and skin cancer." Shorts, stylish ones with no pockets for me and cargo ones for David so that he could serve as my pack mule, were our daily uniforms at first. After four or five days, temperatures plunged into the 40s, and rain fell almost daily. Having brought only summer clothing with us, we rushed to Eugene's J. C. Penney and shopped for long pants and sweaters. To shield ourselves from downpours, we dashed to Cabela's in Springfield, Oregon, and bought ankle-length camouflage ponchos more appropriate for a duck blind than for a sports stadium.

Along with thousands of other spectators, for the two weeks of the Trials, David and I were engrossed in the competition. Thrilled by the athletes' electrifying feats, we jumped up and down and stomped, along with other nearby spectators, so forcefully that our section of the stands shook and rattled as we watched Bernard Lagat win the 5,000-meter race; Matthew Centrowitz, the 1,500-meter race; Allyson Felix, the 400-meter race; and front-running Molly Huddle, the 5,000-meter and the 10,000-meter races. One afternoon as the stands wobbled, I asked a man in a green University of Oregon t-shirt who sat next to me, "Is this thing going to collapse?" Deadpan, he responded, "Feels like it."

Historic Hayward Field was not the setting of my most memorable experience during this trip, though. On our third day in Eugene, David and I ran on Pre's Trail, a four-mile wood-chip-and-bark path named in honor of famed University of Oregon runner Steve Prefontaine. Hailed as the greatest US-born distance runner of all time, Pre held American records in a broad spectrum of races, from 2,000 meters to 10,000 meters. When he competed in Europe, he often ran on wood-chip-and-bark courses. Valuing this surface, Pre recommended the creation of a similar course in Eugene. Four months after his 1975 death in an automobile accident, Pre's Trail became a reality.

As we finished our first run on Pre's Trail one morning, I looked up and saw a distinctive stride. A brown man with a bald head bounded toward me. I recognized him although I had seen him run only on television. Softly, his feet hit the ground midfoot and turned over. A man with shoulder-length straight brown hair accompanied him.

I came to a complete stop. Like a giddy school girl, I gushed, "Meb!" The man with the bald head stopped short when he heard me call his name. Even though I violated a cardinal running rule, interrupting someone's run, he was the ultimate gentleman. Smiling broadly, he hugged me warmly although he had never seen me before this chance encounter. I exclaimed, "This is the best moment of my running life." The man accompanying Meb chuckled at my behavior.

As David and I returned to our rental car after this encounter, I bemoaned that I did not have my phone with me during this once-in-a-lifetime encounter so that I could have taken a selfie of me with Mebrahtom (Meb) Keflezighi, winner of the 2014 Boston Marathon, fourth in the 2012 Olympic Marathon, winner of the 2009 New York City Marathon, and second in the 2004 Olympic Marathon. David comforted me.

"You'll always have your memory," he said.

"But no one's going to believe me."

"I'll be your witness."

"As if someone's going to treat your testimony as proof. You're hardly unbiased."

The day after I met Meb, I literally bumped into an African-American history maker, John Carlos, as I meandered through the food and merchandise booths lining the grounds of Historic Hayward Field. John Carlos had been branded as a dissident when he, the bronze-medal winner in the 200-meter race during the 1968 Olympic Games in Mexico City, and Tommie Smith, the American gold medalist in the event, raised their fists in black-power salutes in protest of the wrongs that people of African descent suffered in the US. I garnered proof of our interaction. I had my phone with me, and David took a photograph of John Carlos and me together.

After encountering present and past running greats, I chanced upon the future. David and I had just taken our seats on our flight from Portland to Baltimore when the Lyles brothers—

Noah (then 18 years old) and Josephus (then 16)—strode down the aisle. They were among the last to board the plane. I pounced upon these sprinters who had both competed in the Trials during which Noah broke the US high-school national record for 200 meters. As the brothers walked past my seat, I hopped up and asked them, "May I take a selfie with you?" Surprise mixed with delight registered on their young faces. In sync, they politely responded as one, "Yes, ma'am." As soon as I snapped the photo, I started clapping my hands. The other passengers followed my lead. A crescendo of applause erupted as they sheepishly walked to their seats.

Self-Deprecation and the Need to Redeem Myself

After David and I returned from the Olympic Trials, I ran in six more races in 2016, a mixture of 5Ks and half marathons. These races were all part of my preparation for an early 2017 marathon that I hoped I would finish in at least 4:45, ten minutes faster than the 4:55 minimum time that I needed to qualify for the 2018 Boston Marathon.

The first of these races was a 5K that occurred at 10:00 a.m. on a blazing Saturday in August, hardly an ideal time of day or an ideal time of year for a race. I ran because a local fitness center, owned by a young widow who lived in my neighborhood, was the sponsor, and the beneficiary of the funds was a non-profit organization that had provided grief counseling to her children after the sudden death of her husband. I encouraged my 37-year-old next-door neighbor to compete as well. As soon as the race began, both of us struggled on the unfamiliar course, which started with a tough uphill mile. Had I known that the beginning was an ascent, I would not have registered. Despite this challenge, I finished the race in 30:02; my pace was 9:40. I won first place in my age group, which was a broader division made up of women 60 and over because of the small size of the race. I ran faster than all but one woman in the 50-to-59 group. After the race, my next-door neighbor suggested, "Let's do this again next year." Screwing up my face, I replied, "I don't want to run this route ever again." She prodded, "Come on. You got me to do it this year. I want a chance to improve my time." Reluctantly, I said, "Okay. But we've got to run this route again and again so we achieve some muscle memory." She asked, "How often?" I countered, "Once each month. By next year this time, we'll have run the course 12 times—or more." This plan came to naught.

She abandoned running and replaced it with online Zumba classes.

My next race was a half marathon that occurred a month later, in September, on Maryland's Eastern Shore. David and I had run this race two years earlier when we had gone to the wrong starting location and started the race 45 minutes after everyone else had begun. This time around, we went to the correct place, but David was injured and did not compete.

On race day, unfortunately, runners were hit with a triple whammy, each portending slower-than-usual times. The temperature was around 80 degrees when the race began. The relative humidity was over 80 percent. The UV index soared as the sun blazed.

Hoping to minimize the impact of these conditions on my performance, I wore all white—visor, sleeveless top, and running skirt. Completing my outfit was a hydration vest containing 24 ounces of water. As soon as I began to run, I took a sip of the already warm liquid. At each water stop, I grabbed two cups of warmer and warmer water and poured them over my head in vain efforts to cool myself. Instead, I poached myself.

At the ten-mile mark, David stood on the edge of the course with two icy bottles of water. He yelled, "Pour one over your head. Pour the other one over the back of your top." I replied, "Thanks, Alberto." He snickered at my homage to Salazar, who famously ministered to his protégé Galen Rupp during the August 2016 Olympic marathon, which we watched on television. David and I laughed as Salazar handed Rupp, the eventual bronze-medal winner, a white hat. We wondered aloud whether Salazar, who was known for using myriad tactics such as pre-race ice vests to give his runners an edge in the heat, had given Rupp an ordinary hat or rather some icy-cold innovation that would lower Rupp's core temperature quickly.

At the eleventh mile, I gained a second wind. After a turnaround at the top of a hill, I sped downward and then ran slightly uphill for about a tenth of a mile before reaching the finish line. As I passed a gasping male runner with dripping blonde hair and a scarlet face, he grumbled, "Who would end a race on an incline?" Invoking my speed work, I ran the last 200 feet at 7:30 pace—lightning fast for me. My overall time of 2:25:46 was close to my worst at this distance. My average pace was an embarrassing 11:07. I was almost as slow as I had been during my first-ever half marathon when my time was 2:27:36 and my pace was 11:16.

Although I won a first-place age-group award, I whined to David about my poor performance. He dismissed my concerns. He said, "It was hotter than hell today." With a sly smile on his face, he added, "It was so tough out there a runner staggered toward the shadow of a chain-link fence." Stunned, I responded. "But the fence is full of holes. It provides no relief from the sun." "My point exactly," he said, chuckling.

As I beat myself up, a woman in her early 50s began to talk with me. She said, "I came in first in my age group, too." *Sotto voce*, she confided, "My time is my absolute worst for a half marathon." The year before, she added, she had run the race in 1:55, but this year she was 17 minutes slower. I told her that I had run the race 15 minutes faster two years earlier. The two of us giggled as we agreed that we should "weather weight" our times. With this adjustment, our times in the past and our times on that scorching hot day, we concurred, were similar. Both of us then decided to give ourselves props for showing up and running when sane people would not have risked heat stroke to win wooden crab-shaped age-group awards. She suggested, "Let's reach over a shoulder and pat ourselves on the back." In unison, we thumped ourselves on our scapulae (wing bones). We crackpots needed our affirmations. In spite of this light-hearted exchange, during the ride from Maryland's Eastern Shore to New

Freedom, I succumbed to self-loathing in which I wallowed for a few days.

A week later, I drove south from New Freedom to the NCR Trail parking lot in Phoenix, Maryland. David followed me in his car. I left my car on the Phoenix lot. Then he drove me to Freeland, Maryland. I ran 18 miles back to the Phoenix parking lot. My plan was that, if I ran well that day, I would compete in a 20 miler on this same surface seven days later. I had registered months earlier when I was running well. After the half-marathon debacle, I felt so vulnerable that I imagined my body, hunched with fatigue, stumbling across the finish mat of the 20 miler in last place. When I emailed Margaret to share my doubts, she responded, "I'm sure you can complete the distance, but you need to have realistic expectations. Just don't put pressure on yourself." I bailed on the 20 miler.

FITTING IN IMMEDIATELY: AN ADDITIONAL RUNNING CLUB

For years, I had paid membership dues to the Baltimore Road Runners Club (BRRC) but had never run with this group. Formed during the early 1970s, the club was sanctioned by the Road Runners Club of America (RRCA), was governed by a board of directors, and provided college scholarships each year to graduating high-school athletes. Consistent with national running trends, most BRRC members were White, male, and well educated. Its recruitment and outreach efforts in recent years had targeted groups underrepresented in running.

The BRRC boasted a veritable platoon of RRCA-certified coaches among its hundreds of dues-paying members, provided 5K and half-marathon training programs free of charge, and offered 30 running events at a range of distances in 2017 when I decided to move beyond just paying dues.

My first active involvement began when I registered for half-marathon training. Speed sessions occurred on Thursday evenings at the same college where I had participated in the training program in 2009 when I prepared for my first-ever race. Endurance runs launched from either Loch Raven Reservoir near Phoenix, Maryland, or from the Sparks, Maryland, parking lot on the NCR Trail.

I was taken aback when, as soon as I entered the track for the first speed-work session, a tall woman with short blonde hair greeted me. "Hello, Marilyn," she said. I was not sure what to make of her calling me by this name. Visibly flummoxed, I was sure, I responded, "No, my name is T. J." By the time that I returned home, I realized that she was confusing me with Marilyn Bevans. Although we were both older African-American women, we looked nothing alike. We were about the same height and weight. She was fairer than I. She never wore makeup when she ran; I wore lipstick and eyeliner. She moved with the assurance of a lifelong athlete. I did not move in this fashion.

Bevans, a Baltimore native, was four years younger than I. Although our paths did not cross until I was in my mid-sixties and she in her early sixties, we had graduated from the same Baltimore public high school and earned bachelor's degrees from the same public college. I knew nothing about her achievements until a woman in the Pacemakers summarized Marilyn's running history in an email to the group. Thus, I learned that Marilyn was the first African-American woman to run a marathon in a time under three hours and the first nationally ranked African-American woman marathoner. When I read *First Ladies of Running* by writer and former marathoner Amby Burfoot, I learned even more—that Marilyn ran in the Boston Marathon six times and finished the race in second place in 1977 behind the legendary Miki Gorman, the only woman to win both the Boston Marathon and the New York City Marathon in the same year. Marilyn's time in 1977 was 2:51:12. That year, *Track and Field News* ranked her as one of the top ten women marathoners in the world. Over the years, she finished 13 sub-three-hour marathons, more than any other US-born woman of African descent.

When I first met Marilyn around 2014, I had no idea that she had such an illustrious racing record. She was running through Druid Hill Park with a few men. I smiled at her as she neared me. I stopped running, and so did she. "Hello," she said. The man who had been running closest to her continued on. I was puzzled. I asked her, "Is that your husband?" Quickly, she responded. "That's one of the guys who run here a lot. I join a bunch of them sometimes." After she introduced herself to me, she laughed and said, "You can remember my name by thinking about our state—Maryland."

I did not talk with her again until months later after a Saturday-morning Pacemakers' run. Marilyn resurrected memories of her running struggles during the 1970s and the 1980s. I stared into her eyes as she recalled the past. I hoped that I did not appear rude. As she talked, I wondered how much faster she would have run had she received more support during her heyday when she shattered the myth that African-American runners were talented primarily as 100-meter or 200-meter sprinters. A full-time public-school physical-education teacher, Marilyn back then ran with the BRRC and coached herself. Sometimes, she had to steel herself during races. From time to time, spectators hurled the "N word" at her with malevolent might as she competed. She ignored them, racking up accolade after accolade. Her accomplishments received national attention when she was inducted into the National Black Marathoners Association (NBMA) Hall of Fame in November 2013 and when she was the focus of an article in the December 2013 issue of *Runner's World*. The NBMA's recognition of her achievements was the first time that I learned of this group's existence. Immediately, I joined the group and wound up shortly thereafter as a member of its roster of achievers—runners who had qualified for and completed the Boston Marathon or who finished marathons in all 50 states or completed all of the marathon majors (Berlin, Boston, Chicago, London, New York, and Tokyo) or finished marathons on all seven continents or achieved in other noteworthy ways.

While reading about the group on its website, I discovered Ted Corbitt, the first African-American man to run in the Olympic Marathon (in 1952). He organized the first ultramarathon in the US. He was one of the founders of the Road Runners Club of America and a co-founder and the first president of the New York Road Runners Club. Ted Corbitt was a prime mover in the effort to certify US race-course distances. Almost superhuman, he was a full-time physical therapist who taught university courses, ran from 100 to 300 training miles per week, and competed in marathons and ultramarathons that were sometimes only a few weeks apart. Like Marilyn Bevans, he endured racial hostility along the way but continued to run, nonetheless.

After the awkward exchange with the woman who called me "Marilyn," I melded with the BRRC. As I waited for the speed session to begin, I gazed panoramically around the track. A fiftyish White woman with long brown hair and a fortyish African-American woman with shoulder-length curly black hair walked slowly as they engaged in an animated conversation. A thin sixtyish African-American woman sporting a blonde Afro ran slowly and steadily. A twentyish white male who appeared to have Asperger's Syndrome sprinted in his own bubble. A pregnant woman of Asian-Indian descent jogged in a determined fashion. Groups of young White women with brown or blonde ponytails chatted and laughed as they warmed up by running around and around the track. Men—old, young, and in between—in a variety of hues circumnavigated the oval.

After everyone warmed up, runners in self-selected pacing groups completed the night's workout—four 400-meter runs. After each 400, the runners briefly jogged or walked. For someone like me who had little sense of pacing, this approach was a godsend.

I ran with a group of about six people at 9:30-per-mile pace. After I ran three of the 400s, Buddy, the RRCA-certified coach who led the program along with Karen, another similarly certified coach, stopped me as I was about to run the last 400 assigned that night. He said, "T. J., if you want to sprint as fast as you can, you have to wait until the workout is over. When you run with your group, you should try to stay around the same pace for each 400. You're running too fast when you get near the end of each 400. Thus, your times are faster than 9:30. You're not meeting the objective." I responded, "Oops." I had been trying to beat everyone else in the group and had paid no attention to pacing consistency.

There was much to be said on the positive side for running with the BRRC not only on the track but also near Loch Raven Reservoir and on the NCR Trail. Two of the major pluses were that, in all contexts, I was encouraged to train properly and to push myself. For instance, during my first run at Loch Raven, I struggled through a hilly five miler with other runners new to the group. I was tired, and I wanted to take a break halfway through, but I did not want to be seen walking. I soldiered slowly on, thus enhancing my endurance and toughening my mind.

When I began to complete long runs with the BRRC, I was already quite familiar with the NCR Trail. Running at Loch Raven was a new experience. What I remember most was not so much the runs but the trips to this destination. During my drives, I frequently saw groups of turkey vultures, large ebony birds with scarlet heads, perched like sentries on utility poles overlooking Interstate 83, the highway on which I drove for 20 miles. Sometimes, they walked purposefully on shoulders bordering the highway. They seemed oblivious to the hundreds of cars and trucks that rumbled by them. From the safety of my car, I shuddered.

One morning near Loch Raven Reservoir, I encountered one of these birds when I did not have my car to protect me. Late, I ran solo. From the dam that controlled the flow of water, white-edged spray rose upward, dampening the air. As I looked skyward, a turkey vulture floated in the air. Its expansive black wings formed a V against the powder-blue canvas. It made wobbly circles. At this point, a trio of women I knew from past runs appeared. I joined them, our group moving in unison.

Our progress was interrupted when a turkey vulture landed softly on the ground near us. "Eek!" I screamed in horror. Felicia, an ebullient runner originally from Ecuador, responded differently. Rapturously, she waxed in her Spanish-inflected English as she gazed at the bird whose wings spanned the breadth of the path. "Es magnífico," she purred. Befuddled, I asked, tactfully I hoped, "You do know that big bird devours carrion?" "Si," she responded. "We need it to clean up our planet. What a miracle that God gave us such a bird."

Methodically, the bird dipped its scarlet head and ripped at an opossum's gray corpse. Bloody, stringy grayish-purple entrails hung like pasta ribbons from its curved beak. The vulture did not bother to look up from its breakfast. Indeed, it did not even move as we trotted by as quickly as we could. I gave the bird a wider berth than did the other women even though I knew on an intellectual level that vultures did not normally attack living creatures.

After our foursome tiptoed around the vulture, Felicia and Georgia, the latter a thirtyish woman originally from Kenya, decided to run an extra uphill mile, but my right hamstring and my right piriformis whined when I began to ascend, so I stopped. I decided that I needed a vacation from hills at least for the rest of the run. As soon as Felicia and Georgia were out of earshot, I said to Kathy, a native Marylander who also opted out of the additional uphill, "I want some of those happy pills that Felicia is taking." Kathy laughed. She responded, "Save some for me." Then she changed her mind about running with me and dashed off, hoping to catch up with Felicia and Georgia. I ran on alone, thinking about how my attitude about the turkey vulture was so different from Felicia's.

A few weeks later, I connected with Kathy again under bird-free circumstances. Both of us ran in a BRRC half marathon, a low-tech old-school run that cost each club member the grand total of $2 and non-members all of $6 to join in the fun. Members were required to participate annually in three of the club's races and volunteer at one club race for eligibility for end-of-year club recognition, usually a performance t-shirt or a running hat emblazoned with the organization's name. I volunteered enough but never ran in enough club events to receive anything.

Without timing chips, the participants in this race inched up to the start and waited for a volunteer to press a button on the top of a handheld air horn, its screeching shattering the early-morning quiet. Taking advantage of my small size and a faux-pleasant smile, I had already elbowed my way to the front. I did not care that I slowed faster people down because I was in their way.

After 13.1 miles, I sprinted across an imaginary finish line. To the right of this spot, with his legs crossed, sat the race director—a middle-aged physician with a mop of dark brown hair, sinewy legs, and a cavalier attitude. He leaned back in a white-and-green webbed lawn chair, the kind with lattice strips and an aluminum frame, and entered finishers' bib numbers and times on a spreadsheet on a laptop computer that he had propped on his thighs. I was surprised that he did not tilt back too far and fall over. He must have balanced his body, the laptop, and the chair exactly right.

After chatting with a few runners about random topics such as the efficacy of knee-high compression socks, current injuries, and their next races, I was about to walk to the rutty parking lot where I had left my car. To reach this destination, I would have to risk my life by traveling up a narrow winding road where drivers of fast cars careened around blind curves before walkers and runners could see their approaches and vice versa. Before departing, I decided to ask some veteran participants about whether an awards ceremony would occur. When they did not know, I asked the race director. Offhandedly, he said, "The after-race activity is eating all these bagels and bananas and drinking all this water." (Because the race was part of the club's series primarily for members, no awards were given, I later learned.) I did not really care that there was no ceremony. I did not come in first in my age group. The top woman runner in the Maryland-

Virginia-Delaware region in my age group finished two-and-a-half minutes before I did. I finished the race in 2:11:58. She finished in 2:09:32. Maybe I should have trained on the course several times instead of showing up that morning without any practice.

Three weeks later, on October 30, 2016, I ran in a half marathon on the Delmarva Peninsula. The race was new to me. After reviewing the results from the year before, I was a bit alarmed initially. I was slow compared to many of the runners in 2015. Then I looked more closely. Apples and oranges! The speedy racers were much younger than I was.

This half marathon began in a tranquil public park that was bordered by a river on whose waters floated iridescent-green-bodied and purple-headed male wood ducks and their gray-brown-bodied and gray-headed female counterparts. Potentially malevolent Canada geese glided nearby. By 9:00 a.m., registrants were lined up to commence the race. The starter's horn shrilly sounded. Approximately 120 half marathoners as well as many 5K racers were on the course. I ran behind at least 80 people. I was not concerned about being so far back. All participants had chips embedded in their bibs.

I had run about 50 feet past the start line when I slowed momentarily to a walk. As the herd approached the park exit where runners were to turn left, a dark-haired woman had toppled headfirst onto the asphalt. Motionless, she appeared to be unconscious. I glanced at her, but the clock had started for me. Every second was precious. Giving her a broad swath, I ran on as did the other participants. During the first mile, I stampeded along with the group with no real sense of how fast I was moving. An hour earlier, I had made the mistake of turning my GPS watch on when I was inside the building where racers picked up their bibs. When I glanced down as I waited in line, a question popped up on my watch's face, "Are you inside or outside?" I entered "inside." When I turned my timer on as I crossed the mat at the start of the race, my watch was confused, and my pace did not register. It thought that I was still inside a building. When I reached a course marker indicating that I had run one mile, desperately, I turned the watch off and then turned it on again. This fix worked. After this point, my pace and distance appeared constantly. Early on whenever I glanced at the watch during the second mile, I saw that I was running too fast. Suddenly, I felt so tired that I contemplated finishing the 5K, occurring also on the course, and giving up on the half marathon. I was not sure that this option was available, so I shuffled along.

My finish time was five minutes slower than my performance in the BRRC half marathon. As soon as I crossed the finish line, I started justifying my time to David. "That race was tough. The elevation map was inaccurate. I didn't anticipate those hills," I moaned. His chin swung from side to side. He was not buying my explanation. He replied, "That course wasn't particularly challenging. You haven't been running as well as you can because you're tired."

A few minutes later, the race director boomed, "It's time to present the awards." After I strode down from a small platform after picking up my age-group award, a giggling curly-haired brunette woman squealed in my direction, "I want to know the name of your plastic surgeon." A short black-haired woman with huge sculpted quads joined the boisterous fun. She said to me, "You're so cute in your little running skirt." The two women tapped plastic cups—with too much force. Both drenched themselves with the frothy dark-brown craft beer that was available gratis to any runner who was willing to stand in a long line in the post-race celebration village.

As I walked away from this festive scene with my award in hand, a middle-aged man said, "You don't look like you're a day over 40." "Forty?" I countered. "Next time you should guess 35."

He laughed. Another man standing nearby savagely spat out, "You're not as old as you claim to be." His venom numbed me.

During the remaining two months of the year, I entered only one more race, a 5K Turkey Trot on Thanksgiving Day 2016. Because the setting of the race was the streets of York City, Pennsylvania, I prepared by training on asphalt rather than on the Trail. Also, I obtained a copy of the course and practiced running on the actual route one weekend. David accompanied me although he did not plan to run in the race. These efforts paid off. I came in first in my age group, which fielded 18 women aged 70 or older, an astoundingly large number for a local race. Other than the Boston Marathon, which attracts an international group of women, I had not run against so many competitors since I aged up to the 70-74 group. My time was 28:52; my pace was 9:17. Amazing since my 5K times had languished around 30 minutes and my pace around 9:45 for years. No mystery about the improvement during the Turkey Trot! I was rested. I focused on running 5K distances at faster speeds in anticipation of this specific race. A clear message was that, even in my dotage, I could race at faster paces when I trained at faster paces.

A Grind: Winter Marathon Training

To run in the 2018 Boston Marathon, I had to complete a qualifying marathon, ideally during spring 2017, when racing conditions should lead to good times. To be ready, I would have to train during the winter. Since the BRRC did not offer sessions during this season, I fell back on a known training option. I forked over $200 for a three-month program provided by the same running store that offered the training for my first race.

The initial training session occurred at night at the same college where I had been introduced to running eight years earlier and where I had participated in the BRRC speed workouts. When I arrived at 6:15 p.m. on the first night, the temperature was about 30 degrees. Darkness enveloped the parking lot. Nearby cars contained silhouettes whose breaths clouded windshields and side windows. As I exited my vehicle, these shapes pushed open their whining car doors. In unison with these shadows, I ran slowly toward the track.

On my left side, I recognized Rebecca, a 30-something woman I met a week earlier when I attended an introductory meeting of the training group at the store.

As we ran, I asked Rebecca, "Can you hear me huffing and puffing?"

"Sure can," she answered.

I had never run after nightfall. My inexperience was probably obvious to the most casual observer. I wore a blinking armband light on my left arm. Running toward oncoming cars on the busy road through the campus, I should have worn the band on my right bicep where it could have been seen easily.

Out of breath as I neared the track, I walked the final 50 or so feet to a grassy area where the coach waited for us runners. After she led us through a ten-minute warm-up, she told us to cover 200 meters as fast as we could. We were to continue this process until we covered this distance six times. After each 200, we were supposed to recover by jogging slowly. After the first 200, I wheezed, gasped, and wheezed again. When the coach saw my distress, she offered me a humongous white inhaler from her first-aid kit. I shrank from using it. Someone's germs were surely on it. To appease her, I held the inhaler about a half-inch from my lips, sprayed the mist into the air, and inhaled as much as I could from that distance. After I was able to talk, I told the coach that the training program was a mistake for me. I explained, "I have exercise-induced asthma, and I won't be able to warm up sufficiently in the cold to run with the group." She replied, "You'll be better off over the long haul because you ran in the cold. Your blood pressure will improve. Just stick with it. I guarantee you that you'll adjust." I was not convinced.

    After I got to know the runners, I was surprised that approximately half of them had paid for running-store training programs multiple times and could have easily formed their own little groups and run together. They liked the amenities and the bonuses of the paid training. Each person received a plan that culminated with her or his marathon. Water stops were in place along training routes. After each weekend long run at Loch Raven or on the NCR Trail, the coach waited for everyone to finish before she departed, so there was no fear of being left behind. When Saturday group runs began from one of the store's locations, a post-training continental breakfast of coffee, orange juice, and bagels greeted runners. On such Saturdays, runners browsed the latest shoes, tops, bottoms, and gear, receiving 25-percent discounts when they made purchases. Participants received a wicking shirt after they completed the program.

I ran with the training group on Saturdays other than when the runs began and ended at the store's downtown-Baltimore location. Instead of joining the group, I ran on the Baltimore and Annapolis (B and A) Trail, where I would run my March 26, 2017, marathon. I needed to build muscle memory!

On the first Saturday that I practiced on the B and A course, David drove me to the high school where the marathon would begin. He planned to run six miles, but I wanted to cover 13 or 14 miles. After running a mile on streets near the school, we entered the B and A Trail at what would be mile 11 of the marathon route. I ran seven miles north, made a U-turn, and ran back south toward the high school.

I looked up and saw a fortyish male member of the BRRC. Startled, I greeted him. He introduced me to his running partner, a woman wearing a 2016 Steamtown Marathon jacket. I rambled about my running in the Steamtown Marathon in 2010 and 2011. They probably remembered these tidbits for as long as I remembered the woman's name. Suddenly, he observed from out of left field, "You've got a really short stride." He looked as though he wanted to say something else about the way that I ran but then "bit his tongue."

I ran with the two of them for a mile or so. Then I slowed down, and they ran on. Unnecessarily, just before I stopped, I explained that I had run about ten miles already when I encountered them. As soon as I threw in the towel, I beat up on myself. When I was a quarter of a mile from the high school, David appeared. I had become warm and had tied my wind jacket around my waist. As soon as I saw him, my jacket loosened as though it had a mind of its own and fell around my knees. I stopped for an instant, pulled the jacket up, tied it tightly, and ran as fast as I could toward him. I hoped that he thought I had run this energetically since we parted ways.

The following week, I ran five days. On Sunday, I ran five slow miles. On Monday, I rested. On Tuesday, I completed a six-mile tempo run. Doubt plagued me. I had begun to self-sabotage. During training runs, I stopped to walk for no reason other than that I momentarily thought about walking.

On Wednesday, I ran with Cynthia, the pretty African-American woman I had met a few years earlier at a 5K, and confessed my destructive behavior to her. She tried to help me. If she saw me slow down, she yelled, "You're not running. Pick up your feet." Her lesson bore fruit—at least on that morning and during much of the following week. On Thursday, I rested. On Friday, I ran three miles before taking a quick tinkle break. Then I ran two more miles without stopping. On the following day, I ran a sixteen miler with the winter-marathon group. Usually, the racing plans that we followed did not include a Friday run followed on Saturday by a long run, but the coach wanted the group to learn how exhausted we would feel at the end of a marathon. To approximate this feeling, we began our long run already tired. I ran slowly, and I took a few walking breaks by design. I did not engage in self-destructive behavior. No miracle. Just determination.

Two weeks later, the temperature was in the mid-twenties according to *www.weather.com* when I began a 20-mile training run at 8:30 a.m. on the B and A Trail. The women's restroom at the community center on whose lot David parked was blazingly hot. I wondered how my body would respond when I went from an inferno inside to arctic conditions outside.

David planned to run a shorter distance than I would, and we agreed to take turns leading for as long as we were together. Because I thought his pace was too fast at the beginning of a run, I volunteered to lead the first mile. We concurred that I would pace myself at 11:00 per mile for the entire distance. I did not honor that promise. I ran the first mile at 10:25 pace. He led the second mile, and I took the third. He was not near me when I finished that mile, so I kept going. After I finished the fourth mile, I ran back to him, and he led the next mile, most of it on a broad bike path near a highway. We descended rapidly for 40 feet or so before U-turning and ascending. After another mile, David returned to the car, and I continued on.

After 20 minutes or so, I was in trouble. One of my woes stopped me in my tracks. I had not been struck by trots in ages. I paid the price for ignoring lessons that I had learned already. Earlier in the morning, I drank too much coffee. I experimented with magnesium because I had read that it helped to convert glucose into glycogen, fuel that I needed to run well. I ignored the warning on the bottle about the laxative effect of this mineral. Compounding the likelihood of the need for urgent defecation, I chewed caffeinated gum from mile one on.

Desperate, I pounced on a man walking toward me. A leashed brown and white beagle trotted alongside him. "Where's the ranger station?" I pled. I knew from past runs that a restroom with porcelain fixtures was located somewhere nearby. Appearing puzzled at first by my obvious distress, he responded, "Two miles up on your left." I could not run or walk that far. I needed to squat immediately in an area from which I could not be seen.

Behind me, a 20-something woman in a fuchsia jacket and black running tights alternated between running and walking. Frequently, her long blonde hair falling forward over her face, she stopped to stretch her hamstrings. A jeans-clad young man with spiky black hair glided on in-line skates alongside her. Whenever I thought that I had reached a point where they could not see me relieve myself, her jacket, like a hound from Hell, appeared yet again. When hope had all but faded that I could elude this couple, I accepted that I would have to soil myself. Then I saw on my right a wooden ramp leading to a narrow path off the B and A Trail. I rushed down the ramp, found a spot behind some bushes in the nick of time, and squatted for about

30 seconds as I nervously looked left and right as well as front and back. Magnesium never crossed my lips again.

I tackled my remaining long runs on the NCR Trail with the winter-marathon group. As we moved along, some shared their race plans. Four members, all women and all first-time marathoners, had registered for the March 11, 2017, Rock and Roll DC Marathon as their first 26.2-mile race. I assumed that they chose this race because of its close proximity to the Baltimore area. No way did I consider this race, though. Two experienced runners, one a young man in his late twenties who ran with the Pacemakers and the other a woman in her early sixties who regularly participated in the BRRC speed sessions, had warned me that the hills on the course were daunting. Reason told me that I had a much better chance of achieving my objective, qualifying for the seventh time for the Boston Marathon, on a flatter and more forgiving course. Curious about the virgin marathoners' thoughts about the Rock and Roll DC Marathon, I asked them, "Have you run sections of the course?" Rebecca, the thirtyish woman who heard my gasps as I struggled to reach the track for the group's first speed session, replied, "I like to be surprised by a race course." I gulped. In addition to dealing with the terrain, on race day, Rebecca and the other first-time marathoners had to overcome another obstacle—the weather. Bitter cold, 26 degrees with wind chills in the teens, greeted them as they crossed the start line. Rebecca did not achieve the finish time that her training runs had predicted nor did the other first timers. Such are the vagaries of the sport.

The following weekend, on March 19, five other members of the group, veteran marathoners, competed in the Shamrock Marathon in Virginia Beach, Virginia. I had been tempted to register for this race, but the same young man who cautioned me about signing up for the Rock and Roll DC Marathon told me to avoid this beachfront marathon because of the unpredictable winds along the Atlantic shoreline. True to this dire prediction, on race morning, 25-mile-per-hour gale-force winds greeted runners. Also, they suffered through pelting rain and sleet. Despite these conditions, after crossing the finish line, a man from the training group waxed rhapsodically via text about how much he enjoyed the race although his fingers were partially frozen, hypothermia was imminent, and his pace was closer to a turtle's than to a hare's. Maybe the cold brought on delirium.

GOOD FORTUNE: MY EIGHTH MARATHON

On B and A Marathon morning, like a matador who dons a *traje de luces* (suit of lights), I ritualistically put on my tried-and-true marathon outfit: a black running skirt; a lime sleeveless top; lime and black ankle-high compression socks; black lightweight gloves; black sleeves; my lucky green sports bra; and the lucky green-and-black cap that I had placed on my head so often that its inner lining was in shreds.

On the eve of the marathon, the weather had been unseasonably hot. From early morning through noon, the temperature was in the low 70s, horrific racing conditions. On marathon morning, though, good fortune smiled on us runners. The sky was overcast. The temperature was in the 40s. I was so cold that I shivered as I waited to cross the start mat.

Calmly, I began to run, pacing myself carefully. As planned, I completed the first 13.1 miles in two hours and 15 minutes. I hoped that I could hold this pace for the second half of the marathon and finish in the neighborhood of four hours and 35 minutes. I ran accordingly until I reached the twentieth mile when my energy waned. At that point, I yogged (ran slowly) for a mile and then surged for a half-mile to energize myself as the coach suggested that the group do whenever we needed to fight fatigue late in the race. This approach helped me to return to my target pace of 10:30 for a mile or so. Then I tired so much that I alternated between walking and running. I laughed at myself. I was "kinda sorta" using the Galloway method (alternations between walking and running), but my alternations were random instead of planned. My finish time was 4:47:38. Although I finished seven minutes faster than the minimum

2018 Boston-Marathon qualifying time for my gender and age, I was disappointed. I had hoped to run faster.

A little over five months later, I applied for acceptance to the Boston Marathon. On Wednesday, September 20, 2017, I received an email that read as follows: "Congratulations! This is to notify you that your entry into the 122nd Boston Marathon on Monday, April 16, 2018, has been accepted, provided that the information you submitted is accurate." Within the next few weeks, in a pile of catalogs, credit-card offers, and other junk mail, my formal acceptance letter arrived in hard-copy form. I hoped that I would have the courage to have fun, understanding that as David often reminded me, "You don't have a shoe contract at stake."

Impulsively Joining an Online Running Group

More than 12 months would transpire between the March 2017 B and A Marathon and the April 2018 Boston Marathon. I hoped to run another full marathon in the interim.

With three other BRRC members, I began to train for a fall 2017 marathon. Buddy, the same coach who co-led the BRRC half-marathon program, was the only man in our little group. In his 50s, he aspired to a 3:30 finishing time in what would be his fourth marathon. The other women were in their 30s. One of them had run in two marathons already and aspired to a time of 4:15 while the other woman was a marathon newcomer and hoped to finish in 4:30. The oldest person as usual, I hoped to run my marathon in 4:45—slower than most of my 26.2 races but faster than my last two.

All of us decided to run local races. The three of them registered for the hilly Baltimore Marathon scheduled on October 21, 2017. The course wound up and down rough-and-tumble asphalt that I knew well because of the numerous times that I had run sections of the route on Saturday mornings with the Pacemakers a few years earlier.

I targeted the Potomac River Run Marathon scheduled a week after the Baltimore Marathon. The timing was perfect for me. The temperature should be ideal, probably in the 40s. The race cost me a nominal processing fee of $10; I had a deferral from the previous year when I bailed because fatigue prevented me from training properly. I knew the course, the C and O Towpath, well, having run the 2014 version of the race.

Unfortunately, training with this small group proved difficult. They usually ran in a suburban-Baltimore neighborhood that was about 25 miles from New Freedom. Spending money on gas and spending time on driving consumed too much of my resources both financial and physical. I followed the plan that Coach Buddy prepared for me, but I trained alone in New Freedom or on the Trail. Usually, for my long runs, I ran south from New Freedom, and David drove to pick me up at an agreed-upon parking lot just off the Trail.

After a month or so, I joined an online running group after participating in a free webinar. I told myself that I would try the program for a month. The cost was $40 per month for a month-by-month subscription. Then someone from the online program telephoned me, and I allowed myself to be persuaded to join for a year—prepaid, of course. Instead of spending $480 per year as a month-to-month member, I would pay $400 as an annual member; two months were in essence free. How could I resist the savings? In hindsight, I realized that I had fallen for a common up-sell ploy.

After I submitted my recent race times as well as information about my age, gender, and training objectives to the coaching staff, I received a marathon plan that I substituted for the one that Coach Buddy had given me. There was a high level of individual accountability; I uploaded my workouts, including information such as distances and paces achieved. From time to time, I uploaded photographs of scenes from my runs. I received feedback not only from one of a bevy of coaches but also from other runners worldwide who followed me. The other runners encouraged me, and I did the same for them. I thought of them as buddies although I never met any of them face to face. Also, through my membership in the group, I had access to a plethora of online articles and podcasts on almost every imaginable running topic.

Ouch! A Run-Stopping Injury

"Oh! No!" During a 12-mile run, I felt a sharp pain in my left foot. I could barely run, but I moved along, nonetheless. As I ran the final mile, I saw David in oversized shorts walking slowly toward me. He had driven to a parking lot near Monkton, Maryland, to meet me and drive me home. As soon as he came within earshot, I shouted, "Are those Bryan's old shorts?" David's face reddened. Bryan had worn these same tan cargo shorts 15 years earlier when he was 20 years old. When Bryan, seven inches taller than David, cast them aside, David grabbed them up although they were too long and wore them when he mowed the lawn. Hobbling, I sped up nonetheless when a teenage boy with dripping brown hair came up next to me. Both the boy and I laughed when I ran faster and faster, trying to match his pace. David grimaced. Firmly, he ordered, "Stop, T. J." I slowed down. I replied, "But I'm a half-mile short." He shook his head and gave me "the lip," a straight tight mouth that bespoke frustration. "You're limping," he said. Grudgingly, I halted. I leaned on him as I slowly made my way to his car.

When I told an online coach about my injury, he recommended that I rest for a few days. I talked with my chiropractor about the problem, and she administered electrical stimulation to my left foot. This treatment had no impact on the pain. I stretched my calves. I iced my foot four times daily. I foam rolled my lower left leg. When none of these approaches alleviated the pain, I made an appointment with my podiatrist, who informed me that once again I had plantar fasciitis. At least the injury was an equal-opportunity one. In 2013, my right foot was injured. As a precaution, he prescribed physical therapy for both feet this time around, not just the affected left foot.

During my down time from running, I read about the sport. Vicariously, I raced alongside the Tarahumara (Ruramuri) tribespeople of northern Mexico's Copper Canyon in Christopher McDougall's *Born to Run* (2009). I "rode the pain" as I matched Frank Shorter step for step in his *My Marathon: Reflections on a Gold Medal Life* (2016).

Additionally, every other day, I attempted to retain some actual semblance of cardiovascular fitness by riding my bike, which David placed on a trainer in our basement. Twice weekly, I rushed into a local physical-therapy facility where I stretched my calves on a slant board, completed toe curls with a towel, and massaged my plantar fascia with a frozen water bottle. So that I would not experience the excruciating morning pain associated with the tightening of the plantar fascia while I slept, I attempted to wear a night splint and was no more successful than I had been in the past. After a half-hour of sleeplessness, it lay next to me until I kicked it onto the floor where I stumbled over it when I rushed in darkness to the bathroom during the night. Since some studies suggested that taping the foot might relieve the morning pain, every night David affixed adhesive strips to the bottom of my injured foot. In three months, I recovered from plantar fasciitis, a relatively brief period when I thought about how long I did not run the first time that I dealt with this condition. Perhaps I had been a wimp in 2013 and could have run much sooner than I did.

During this running hiatus, I tried to identify the causes of my bouts of plantar fasciitis. I wondered whether I was paying the price for a lifetime of wearing three-inch heels every single workday. I probably spent approximately 90,000 hours in these "towers" over the more than 40 years that I had been employed.

Through my readings, I learned that, over the long term, women who wore high heels developed more frequent occurrences of ankle and knee arthritis than did women who avoided such footwear. High-heel wearers experienced more instances of plantar fasciitis. A lack of arch support was the cause. They developed more incidents of toe changes such as corns, calluses, bunions, and hammer toes. Narrow toe boxes were the cause. They experienced greater shrinkage and stiffness of the Achilles tendon. Unnatural foot positioning was the cause.

For me, corns on my baby toes caused constant pain back when I wore high heels. I grimaced and groaned but continued to wear such shoes nonetheless because I believed that my legs looked more attractive in them, a truth borne out by research studies that indicate that wearing high heels elongates the leg and enhances the appearance of a woman's derriere. Also, studies showed that wearing high heels changed a woman's gait by reducing her stride length as well as increasing her hip rotation and hip tilt in ways deemed attractive.

While wearing high heels might have been one of the long-term factors, the immediate cause of my most recent bout of plantar fasciitis was probably a radically different type of footwear. A week before my brief duel with the wet-haired runner, my feet reached a tipping point as a result of a chain of missteps. I wore one-inch sling-back heels when David and I traveled by bus from the Baltimore suburbs to New York City to see *Kinky Boots*, a Tony-winning musical. The shoes had always seemed comfortable when I walked in them in the past. However, shortly after we disembarked at New York City's Rockefeller Plaza, fluid-filled toe blisters brought me to a halt. Limping into a nearby store plastered with posters advertising a shoe sale, I bought a pair of wedge-heeled sandals with a metal adornment that deeply gashed the tops of my feet a few minutes after I slipped them on. Sticky red droplets oozed from the area. Forty-five dollars wasted. Next, I went inside another nearby store and purchased a pair of flip flops for $12. I knew wearing such footwear was dangerous and could lead to increased clumsiness, heel pain tied to accentuated heel-strike impact, increased toe effort that could result in hammertoe, blisters, strained or overextended Achilles tendons, and exposure to bacterial and fungal infections as well as other negative consequences. My thinking was that I would not be walking much; thus, the risks were minimal. I was dead wrong.

As soon as I placed the flip flops on my feet, David and I hurried four or five blocks to a Turkish restaurant for a lunch of salmon and rice with chickpeas. Thinking ahead to our next meal, which we would consume on the bus on the way back to Maryland, we searched, for 45 minutes, for a tiny Mom-and-Pop Chinese-dumpling shop that we visited six months earlier when we saw the musical *Get On Your Feet* on Broadway. The steamed and fried dumplings—fish stuffed, vegetable stuffed, and shrimp stuffed—were so scrumptious that just thinking about a repeat of this meal caused me to drool. In anticipation, I dabbed the corners of my mouth. The deleterious effects of walking so long and so far in flip flops were not even a remote thought.

After completing seven weeks of physical therapy after my flip-flops mistake, I began training once more. Upon my return to running, I stood on my tiptoes, rooted around our garage, and pulled my orthotics down from a shelf lined with at least six pairs of never-worn or once-worn running shoes that I rejected after purchasing them. After pounding the orthotics against my thighs to loosen the dust that had accumulated, I inserted them inside my running shoes that day and every single day on which I ran. I followed this course of behavior even though I wondered whether orthotics might be analogous to snake oil.

CAREFULLY PREPARING FOR THE 2018 BOSTON MARATHON

To prepare for the April 2018 Boston Marathon, I registered for a February 2018 half marathon in Hilton Head, South Carolina. I selected this race because it occurred halfway through my 18-week marathon schedule and because David and I had run well in this half marathon two years earlier. This time around, David was unable to train because of a lingering cold. His sole role was to be my one-person crew.

Up until the gun boomed to signal the half marathon's start, I wanted to bail. I felt underprepared. I had missed training sessions because of freezing rain, ice, and snow that imprisoned me inside for days and days. My body had no time to adjust to the South-Carolina weather, which was radically different from the 20-degree conditions in New Freedom, Pennsylvania. The temperature at the half marathon's start was 61 degrees and would rise.

Changing my mind was not an option. We had traveled about 650 miles in two days and had spent money on hotels and restaurants. Also, I had subjected David to stress and fatigue. On race morning, I wanted to arise by 4:45 a.m. so that I would be ready to run at 8:00 a.m. David could not set the alarm on the broken clock radio in our hotel room. He both set his sports-watch alarm and requested a wake-up call from the hotel's guest-services department. The following morning, his eyes were dull, and his mouth sagged. After I accused him of looking tired, he admitted, "I was so worried that I wouldn't get you up in time to get ready for the race that I couldn't sleep."

I finished the half marathon in 2:14:15. My pace per mile was a disheartening 10:14 (25 seconds slower per mile than my 9:49

pace in 2016 when the temperature and humidity had been much lower). Searching for consolation, I compared my results with those of women and men near my age. I was first of four women in the 70-74 age group; faster than all nine women finishers in the 65-69 age group; faster than 13 of 17 women finishers in the 60-64 age group; and faster than 29 of 34 women finishers in the 55-59 age group.

Also, I ran more quickly than did a large number of men close to my age. I was faster than four of five finishers in the 70-74 male group; faster than seven of ten finishers in the 65-69 male group; faster than nine of 14 finishers in the 60-64 male group; and faster than 14 of 27 finishers in the 55-59 male group. At this point, I stopped my compulsive comparisons.

After David and I returned home from the half marathon, I returned to the marathon-training plan provided by the online-training program. I vowed to heed the online coaches' teachings about the long slow run. They said that this pace should be between 55 to 75 percent of a runner's 5K pace. Ideally, the pace should be 65 percent. I provided my most recent 5K pace, which was 9:17 per mile, and a coach determined that my optimal long-run pace should be between 11:00 to 11:45 per mile. I had not moved so slowly since my first 12 months as a runner. I would have been crawling had I submitted my usual 5K time of 9:45. The coach explained that such slow running increased the number of red blood cells and the amount of hemoglobin and oxygen that these cells could carry to the muscles. More oxygen enabled the muscles to convert greater amounts of fat, protein, and glycogen into energy. Even after the coach repeatedly told me to pace myself in accordance with this formula, I had been so brainwashed that speed ruled that I continued to run faster than prescribed. Additionally, adhering to this slower pace was difficult when I ran with others whose paces were faster than mine. If I ran as slowly as I should, they would leave me. They would think that I could not run faster, and I would feel humiliated.

The online-coaching staff told us runners that the longest runs need not be 20 miles or more. We should not exceed three hours. Beyond this time, little significant endurance gains were to be had. The cutoff for people running more than ten minutes per mile was 16 miles. Like the tyranny of speed, long runs of 20 or 22 miles had been firmly fixed in my mind. Contrary to the coaches' advice, I ran 20 miles twice as I prepared for the 2018 Boston Marathon. These runs lasted more than three and a half hours.

To ensure that my nutrition was such that I would have enough glycogen for fuel during the marathon, I emulated as much as possible the eating habits of Kenya's Eliud Kipchoge, often heralded as the greatest marathoner of the modern era. He ate carbohydrate- and nitrate-rich foods such as ugali (a cornmeal, millet flour, and sorghum dish that is a staple of Kenyan runners); green leafy vegetables; kidney beans; Kenyan tea; eggs; and milk. No ugali for me! However, I did chow down on oatmeal with fat-free milk at breakfast time. I ate spinach, broccoli, kale, red-bean curry, and a small piece of seafood for dinner followed by a custard for dessert that was my way of ingesting eggs and milk. During the day, I drank cups and cups of ginger tea.

I tested a marathon brew that one of the online coaches developed: a mixture of water, rice starch, beet powder, and beta alanine. Proving more stomach friendly than commercial gels, this blend became my go-to nutrition as I prepared for the 2018 Boston Marathon.

Badass Running: The 2018 Boston Marathon (My Ninth Marathon)

David and I arrived in Boston on the evening of Saturday, April 14, 2018. We had arranged our hotel through Marathon Tours. Left to our own devices, we would have chosen a place that was much more basic and that cost much less than we paid for these accommodations. As we waited to check in, we realized that we were staying in the same hotel as were some elite athletes past and present. Legendary marathoner Bill Rodgers stood behind us in line. No shrinking violet, I pounced on him and introduced myself. After David and I checked in, we encountered Somali-American distance runner and five-time Olympian Abdihakem "Abdi" Abdirahmani as he waited for friends with whom he was going to dinner. After chatting with him for a few minutes, I literally bumped into the wheel chair of Russian-American Tatyana McFadden, winner of multiple World Marathon Majors' push-rim races, as she exited an elevator as David and I attempted to enter. Unlike my encounter with Meb, my interactions with each of them were captured in photographs, a bit blurry, that David took with my phone. I should have cleaned the lens.

On the following day, David and I exited our hotel intent on reaching the race expo and picking up my bib as quickly as possible.

"Oh, no!" I squealed as soon as the hotel door closed behind us.

"What's wrong?" David asked as he turned toward me.

Feeling my head, I said, "My lucky cap! It just blew off my head."

As David and I tried to catch the fleeing cap, a middle-aged woman wearing a mottled black-and-white Cossack hat walked nearby with a small silky white dog in tow. Loudly, she said to me, "This is a wind tunnel." Then pulling her resisting pooch behind her, she hurried into the street to join us in the cap chase. A taxi driver saw the scenario as it unfolded. He stopped his yellow cab alongside a silver Honda Accord under which my lucky cap with the shredded lining had found refuge from the wind. Holding up traffic, he said in a Caribbean accent, "There it tis." He pointed under the Honda. David rushed over and grabbed my hat before the wind could pick it up again.

As we traipsed to the expo, icy rain pummeled us, and frigid winds gusted. I hoped that the weather would improve overnight, but it did not. On Monday, April 16, David and I awakened to the coldest Boston-Marathon conditions in 30 years—temperatures at the start around 38 degrees, pelting arctic rain falling from the gloomy-gray sky, and headwinds that reached 35 miles per hour and slowed runners' progress toward the finish line.

Because I wanted to spend the minimum amount of time in Hopkinton, I boarded one of the last buses to the athletes' village. I knew that the tents would be so teeming with participants that securing even the smallest space in which to stand or sit would be a challenge. I hoped that someone would defer to me because of my age and gender, fear of African Americans, or a mixed bag of these elements.

I arrived in the village 15 minutes before my group was scheduled to begin at 11:15 a.m. I needed to tinkle. What a surprise. Reaching a porta-potty safely was slow going because of the dangerously slippery mud that contradictorily reminded me both of melted milk chocolate and diarrheal feces. The wrong step and I would plop down into this slop. Tentatively, I plodded to the porta-potties one, two, three, and four times. From time to time, the muck tried to suck my shoes off. But I fought back and unstuck them. After my final trip to a potty, I attempted to change into dry shoes and socks that I had brought with me in a plastic trash bag and to tie the strings of my capris, which I had unloosened while in the first porta-potty and let hang loose until I made my last pit stop. Even though I wore gloves, my hands were so cold by this time that they did not function. I wished that I had brought hand warmers with me. I had at least four packs at home in the back end of my car. Seeing my plight, a woman with a gentle smile on her face and a volunteer badge on her black puffer coat walked over to me.

"Do you need help?" she asked.

"I can't switch my wet shoes with my dry ones. My hands are so cold they don't work."

I leaned on her. Stabilizing me, she stood like a post as I stood unsteadily on one leg as I changed each shoe.

Finally, I walked to the start line. Everyone had gone. The only person I saw on the course during the first mile was a woman wearing a large yellow bib with the number 85 on it. I did not learn until later that she was Katherine Beiers and that her bib number matched her age. She was the oldest woman to complete the marathon that day. Her time, I learned later, was 7 hours and 50 minutes.

For some reason, all that I could think about as I began was what I had read about the 1963 Boston Marathon during which weather conditions were similar. Ethiopian Abebe Bikila, the 1960 Olympic Marathon and later the 1964 Olympic Marathon champion, had run the Boston Marathon and endured headwinds, frigid rain, and high winds foreign to his usual running conditions. Some observers of the 1963 race thought that not only the weather but also Bikila's too-fast running of the first half of the Boston Marathon had doomed him. Bikila finished in fifth place; this marathon was the single international 26.2-mile race that he did not win. As my mind hopped around, I forced myself to avoid thoughts about Bikila's performance. What did his run have to do with me? I was hardly an elite athlete at my peak. I was an old-lady runner without a peak. I laughed.

Next, I began to worry about my body. Although I had inhaled Albuterol on the bus to Hopkinton, I feared that exercise-induced asthma might surface and hamper me. Perhaps fear blended with adrenaline settled my breathing that morning. Wearing a purple-and-tan camouflage running jacket, my least favorite outer garment and hence one that I was most willing to sacrifice, I sprinted through the first half mile, alarmed that I was probably the last person to begin the race. Warm by then, I could tolerate the jacket no longer. At home, I had separated the sleeves and the lining from the outer shell with scissors. Like a superheroine, I ripped the jacket smoothly from my body as I sped along. I had practiced this move in the hotel. I calmed down and settled into the pace, around 10:20, that I planned to run.

I finished the first half of the marathon in about two hours and 15 minutes, almost the same time in which I had completed the first half of other marathons. Along the way, I willed myself to conjure up pleasant thoughts that brought smiles to my face. I had read a study that posited that smiling, even faux smiling, improved running efficiency and lowered perceived exertion. Also, smiling yielded, the study stated, a positive mindset, important because the sport was a mental game as well as a physical activity. Another article claimed that the efficacy of smiling was embraced to such an extent that even the great Kipchoge used this approach. I suspected that, with a fake smile plastered on my face, I looked like a wincing idiot.

I adhered to my pacing plan until I reached mile 15. Excruciating pain in my right foot stopped me for a few seconds. I planned to plop two of the extra-strength aspirin that I had placed in my water belt into my mouth. When I unzipped the belt, what I found there were granules. A rotund man in a lime-green rain coat with "Volunteer" plastered across its front stared at me as I licked my right index finger and picked up bits of the white powder and swallowed. I wondered whether he thought I was doing a line of cocaine. Although he said absolutely nothing to me, I explained, "This is just extra-strength aspirin."

The agony continued. I ran through the deepest puddles of the coldest rain, hoping that the water would ease the agony. When this approach failed, I searched for a medical tent. As soon as I spotted one, I rushed there and pulled back the flap. Rain had collected near the opening, and my vision was momentarily obscured as I underwent a chilling baptism.

Holding an electronic tablet in his hand, a tall man who appeared to be the head volunteer strode toward me. He typed my bib number in a space on the screen.

He asked, "How can we help you?"

I responded, "Can I get an aspirin here?"

"We don't have any medication. You might be able to get something at the next tent."

I was befuddled by his answer, for I thought that all the tents were similarly stocked with medicines and similarly staffed with personnel.

My confusion was no doubt clear on my face.

"What exactly is wrong?" he asked.

"My foot feels as though it's broken in half."

He typed again on the tablet. Then he called another man over. This other man, I quickly learned, was a physical therapist. Fortunately, for me, no other runners were waiting for his help. I sat on a cot and pointed to the middle of my right foot. To him, I speculated that plantar fasciitis was the culprit. The physical therapist said, "If you had plantar fasciitis, the pain would most likely manifest itself more in your heel. You're pointing to your arch. I'll tape it."

After about 20 minutes that seemed like 20 days, I stood up. Hot air from a heater had been directed at me the entire time that I had been inside. Also, warming the space were other heaters around which runners who could not go on had huddled. Cold air entered the tent every time someone entered or exited. Because I had stopped for such a long time and cooled down, I shivered uncontrollably as I put on my right sock and my right shoe, which had been nonsensically drying in front of a heater the entire time that I was in the tent. They would both be soaking wet as soon as I stepped outside. The physical therapist encouraged me to wrap a metallic warming blanket around my shoulders before I left. To ensure that the fierce winds did not blow it off, he cut a piece of tape from a spool and gently fastened the blanket around my neck. Now I had a cape. Twice a superheroine in the same race. Panicked because I had lost so much time, I zoomed out of the tent. A caramel-colored woman wearing no hat or cap in deference to the icy rain sped past me as I stepped onto the course. I could not see her face. I zeroed in on a tiny thinning spot on the crown of her head. Mesmerized, I ran slightly behind her like a stalking thoroughbred. I lasted only about a mile at this pace. At 10:04, this mile was my fastest.

I returned to my plan of running around 10:20 pace. I chugged along. I looked up and glanced at the iconic CITGO sign, the gasoline company's red triangle against a white background signaling since 1965 that the race's end was near. Fueled by fear, I ran as fast as I could, probably about 10:30 pace. I looked for the finish line but saw it nowhere. Desperately, I asked a thin brunette woman who ran near me, "How much farther?" She gasped, "You'll see the finish line when we make a left onto Boylston Street." When we turned, I was aghast. All over the street were piles of discarded plastic garbage bags and cast-off rain ponchos. Runners had torn their rain and wind protection from their bodies so that their bib numbers would be visible to the finish-line announcer and to the finish-line photographers whose company would later attempt to sell memories. Tentatively, I wove through this obstacle course. Now and then I stumbled when I adjusted my pace or direction too late to negotiate the small mounds. Fortunately, I retained enough balance to remain erect.

As the finish line drew nearer and nearer, I tore away my metallic warming blanket and added it to the heaps on the wet street. The finish-line announcer exclaimed, "Crossing the finish line now is T. J. Bryan from Pennsylvania." I could muster not an iota of enthusiasm as I heard my name. I was simply glad that the race was over.

Woozy. Thirsting for an IV. Wanting a wheelchair. No medical volunteers nearby. In my two past Boston Marathons, a throng of smiling women and men triple teamed finishers and foisted medals on them. This time around, no volunteers were in sight. When I encountered a man who seemed to know his way around the finish area, I asked him, "Where're the finishers' medals?" He pointed toward an innocuous black van, where, unceremoniously, someone handed me a royal blue and yellow medal.

I trudged to my hotel, which was about a half-mile away. Because I had a long history of being directionally challenged, David and I had practiced this walk the day before to ensure that I knew my way back. We knew that by the time that the race ended, he would be on a flight home. He had to meet his "dumplings," the term he affectionately used for his mathematics students at the university where he had been teaching on a part-time basis for the last three years, for a class on Tuesday morning.

I left a trail of wet footprints from the hotel entrance to the elevator and to my room. I remembered that I was staying in room 256. Hooray! That morning, I had feared that I would forget and have to slosh to the front desk for help.

As soon as I entered the room, I grabbed the remote from a bedside table and turned on the television. A Boston-area sports commentator told the viewing audience that a US woman and a Japanese man had won, a shocking occurrence given that athletes from Kenya or Ethiopia had usually come in first during the last 20 years. The US woman was Desiree Linden (née Davila), who finished in 2:39:54, the slowest winning time for a woman since 1978. This was the same woman who came within seconds of winning the Boston Marathon in 2011, the year of my first Boston Marathon. The man was Yuki Kawauchi, whose winning time of 2:15:58 was the slowest for a man since 1985.

I rushed to the phone in my room and placed a room-service order. I groaned when the person at the other end of the line told me that I had to wait 45 minutes for the meal to arrive. In the interim, I showered for at least 30 minutes. I was frozen to the bone. When the tray finally arrived, I was so ravenous that, after I inserted a serrated knife into a warm loaf of bread sprinkled with rosemary and chunks of sea salt and slathered it with honey butter, I bit my tongue as I devoured the first slice. I wolfed down steaming New England clam chowder and chugged a frosty glass of Viognier.

I was in no hurry to check my race results. I knew that I had not qualified for the 2019 Boston Marathon. I had no plans to register even had I qualified, but I would have embraced achievement at such a level.

Removing the tape from my right foot moved to the top of my agenda. The adherent that the physical therapist sprayed on the bottom and top of my foot was so effective that I could not peel off the tape. Without scissors, I resorted to the serrated knife that I had used to slice my bread; it was still tacky with honey butter.

As I sawed through the tape, my cell phone signaled a text message. Cynthia wrote, "Your time was good." Huh? I was puzzled. I clicked on the race website. My time was cited as 4:08. I knew that this was incorrect. When I checked again the next morning, it had been changed to 5:55. This time was incorrect, too. Immediately, I saw the reason for this most recent error. My first 5K was incorrectly recorded as taking 80 minutes. I knew that I had run it in about 30 minutes.

A new mission. I planned to email and telephone the Boston Athletic Association every single workday until my results were corrected. When revised, my official time was 5:06:44—close to 12 minutes slower than the minimum time of 4:55 that would have qualified me for the 2019 Boston Marathon. My loss of approximately 20 minutes in the medical tent reminded me yet again that, like life, anything can happen on any given day.

After I returned home, I learned the full impact of the harsh weather on runners. More than 2,500 runners sought attention in medical tents along the course. A total of 1,123 of 29,979 runners did not finish.

Overall, a larger percentage of men, five percent of the total male participants, dropped out. A smaller percentage of women, 3.8 percent, did not finish. Some researchers attributed women's greater persistence to several factors. Women's higher body fat enabled them to handle cold weather better than men did, and women's inherently higher pain-tolerance level, tied to their ability to withstand childbirth, enabled them to handle discomfort better than men did. These factors were at play even in radically different weather conditions, such as the heat of the 2012 Boston Marathon when women dropped out at lower rates than did men. Another factor, according to experts, was the difference in the genders' decision-making patterns. In general, women paced themselves better than did men and adjusted their expectations based on race conditions more readily than did men.

The brutal conditions defeated 23 elite runners. The DNF list included former Boston Marathon champions and a former Boston Marathon runner-up: Lemi Berhanu, who finished first in 2016; Lelisa Desisa, who finished first both in 2013 and 2015; Caroline Rotich, who finished first in 2015; and Galen Rupp, who finished second in 2017. Other elites who did not finish included Philemon Rono, winner of the Scotiabank Toronto Waterfront Marathon in 2016 and 2017 and American master's runner Deena Kastor, bronze medalist in the 2004 Olympic Marathon, winner of the 2005 Chicago Marathon, and winner of the 2006 London Marathon.

Predictably, core runners also succumbed to the merciless weather. Surprise was too weak a word to capture my response when I learned after I returned home that good runners I knew did not finish the race. Already, I knew that one such runner, a top age-group winner in the Baltimore area, had not crossed the finish line. I had encountered her around mile 14 of the race. Out of nowhere, she materialized next to me yelling, "You look fantastic." Like an errant negative thought that explodes mindless happiness, she penetrated my zone. I was annoyed by this intrusion and wished her away. "Abracadabra!" Almost immediately, she vaporized. A week or so after the race, she confided in an email, "I just couldn't get into it. It was sheer torture." To her credit, she did not claim to have experienced hypothermia, which was the explanation du jour.

I defined myself as a badass, as someone who did not quit. Thus, I continued the race even though I was injured. Also, I had spent more than $3,000 on the experience: $1,500 for accommodations, $700 for airline tickets for David and me, and close to $1,000 on meals and transportation from and to Logan

Airport and travel within the city of Boston. At the very least, I needed a finisher's medal.

After I returned home, I shared my marathon misadventures with a handful of runners with whom I usually communicated on the online-training site. Abigail was a fortyish scientist who worked and lived in Boston, Massachusetts, and usually ran half marathons. Tom was a retired engineer in his 70s who spent months traveling with his wife around the US in his recreational vehicle. He also ran in the 2018 Boston Marathon. Avi, a retired businessman and a marathoner in his late sixties, lived in Mumbai, India. Teresa, an attorney and trail runner in her 50s, lived outside Washington, DC. Abigal had been worried about how, as an exercise-induced-asthma sufferer, I would deal with the weather conditions. Tom, who crossed the finish line in approximately five hours and 40 minutes, posted about the ill-fitting ski pants that he had worn, so large and loose that they kept falling below his waist and slowing him down. Teresa worried when she saw that I had no recorded time during the first fourth of the race. She posted, "I thought something terrible must have happened." I responded, "My chip didn't register when I crossed the start line." Avi applauded my resolve. An online coach wrote, "What a day! Wow, resilient and enduring on your end to hurdle each of the obstacles you faced!" He captured the essence of what I had learned from this race—the importance of bouncing back and continuing on. He added, "You sure did put it out there, and it was you that won the day, not the course, not the weather."

At this point, my one-year membership in the online program was close to expiring. Although I valued the interactions with my pen pals, I decided I would not continue. Uploading my runs and writing summaries of my experiences as well as responding to other runners' posts consumed more time than I wanted to give. I was unconvinced that my gains as a runner offset the financial and time costs.

A few weeks after the 2018 Boston Marathon, I reflected on my experience. To think that my glass was half full rather than half empty seemed trite, but I did feel grateful. I had lucked upon a medical tent with a physical therapist inside. Also, I had not bonked (experienced sudden fatigue because of a lack of glycogen), perhaps because of the long slow runs. Maybe my consumption of nitrate-rich food kept me more energized than I had been during past marathons. Maybe the coach's marathon brew had kept me going. Or maybe the rest break in the medical tent had been the determinant.

Limping after I returned to New Freedom, I sought out a podiatrist closer to my home than was the podiatrist who had treated me for about five years. A former running zealot who had blown out an ankle and had become embittered about the sport, the new podiatrist lectured me, "You have a torn plantar fascia. You should have stopped as soon as your foot began to ache." Incredulous, I responded, "I trained for months. You can't be serious." Then he shook his head in disbelief. In a toxic voice, he responded, "You're an addict." Suddenly, he inappropriately stared at me from the top of my head to my feet and said, "You look like you're in your forties." Then, dismissively, he ended our interaction and asked me to wait for an arch pad that one of his medical assistants would make for me. He sent me on my unhappy way.

I returned to my former podiatrist who prescribed physical therapy for both feet yet again. My first impulse was to return to the same physical therapist who months earlier had treated my left-foot plantar fasciitis; his office was close to my home. Then I remembered how abruptly he booted me from therapy even though I told him that my foot still hurt.

Unwilling to risk such treatment again, I searched the web for another physical therapist close to me. At the new place, the therapist was Suzanne, a fast-walking fiftyish blonde who had been a soccer player from her teenage years through her forties.

After an evaluation that included measurements of my range of motion and a gait analysis, she summed up the state of my lower body in a few words: "You're a mess." Then she asked me, "Why do you abuse your body like this?" This must have been a rhetorical question. Surely, she knew the answer after interacting with myriad runners during her 20-year career. Then, grabbing my right foot, she placed her thumb on the sole near the ball and her index finger on the top and squeezed them together. Rat-a-tat-tat! "Your feet are weak. Look! I can feel my thumb and the finger through your flesh. You don't have much musculature." She recommended that I strengthen my feet by completing doming exercises (pressing my toes downward into the floor while keeping my heel planted to form a mound). She recommended that I do towel curls (scrunch a towel toward me with my toes). She suggested calf raises to strengthen heel tendons and calf muscles that support the arch. Next, Suzanne said that my gluteals were underactivated. My adductors were overworked. My hips were not balanced. My right leg was longer than my left leg. At the time, I did not know that leg-length discrepancy was fairly common. She adjusted my right leg manually, and a minute later it fell back into its habitually longer-than-left-leg position. A major reason for this discrepancy, she said, was that my right hip was internally rotated. Later, as instructed, I completed Pilates circles to address this discrepancy. In the long term, they were no more effective at eliminating my leg-length differences than were Suzanne's manual adjustments.

She explained that all the problems she rattled off were causes of my plantar fasciitis. She said, "I can't make any promises, but you shouldn't be sidelined again because of your feet if you perform the exercises I teach you." I hoped she was right. She handed me some sheets describing clamshells (a side-lying exercise to strengthen hips); small-ball squeezes (a side-lying exercise to strengthen hip adductors); and closed-chain stepping (side steps with a band to strengthen hip abductors).

She grabbed some black kinesiology tape and wrapped it in the same pattern on each of my feet, told me to wear shoes with a slight heel, and told me to take a non-steroidal anti-inflammatory drug for inflammation and pain.

I took additional steps. I chucked my orthotics. I had worn them faithfully after my first bout of plantar fasciitis in 2012, but the bottoms of my feet fell apart, nonetheless. When I talked with runner acquaintances who were physical therapists by profession, some of them suggested that I roll the bottom of each foot on a tennis ball daily and ice my feet at least once a day and increase the frequency of icing to twice a day when I experienced the slightest foot pain. After reading an article in the "Your Health" section of the May 2019 issue of the *AARP Bulletin*, I went barefoot when I was at home. The writer argued that wearing shoes deprives feet of sensory stimulation needed to foster movement. Initially, I cringed because I was concerned about my feet becoming dirty or cold. I adjusted quickly, though, and began to luxuriate in using my feet in ways in which they were designed to function.

Because I knew the importance of overall body strength, I continued to perform upper-body exercises that I had learned in fitness classes over the years or that David taught me. Using his Bowflex machine, I performed seated crunches and standing-oblique exercises to strengthen my abdominals, completed seated rows to strengthen my rhomboids, and performed pull downs to strengthen my latissimus dorsi primarily and my biceps and rotator-cuff muscles secondarily. Using free weights, I strengthened my deltoids by completing front and lateral raises, strengthened my biceps and triceps by completing curls and extensions, and strengthened my upper trapezius by completing shoulder shrugs.

Yet Another Injury

By June 2018 when David and I went on a two-week vacation throughout Iberia, I had recovered sufficiently enough from plantar fasciitis that I ran with him in a park in San Sebastian in the Basque region of northern Spain. The plan was that I would run two miles and then walk alone back to the hotel. Unfortunately, we became lost. Finally, after three miles of running and another two miles of walking to find the hotel, we encountered a young man with a cell phone. From the recesses of my mind came a few words of my college Spanish. I asked him, "Dónde está el Silken Amara Plaza?" The man understood me well enough to use his phone to locate the hotel and point us toward it. The morning after this misadventure, intense pain in my pelvic area kept me in bed until David helped me to stand. I struggled to walk to the bathroom, to shower, and to dress. I joined our tour group for a day jammed with sightseeing. Although I could barely move, I smiled and laughed and oohed and aahed. When that interminable day was over, I dreaded going to bed. How much pain would I feel the next morning? I was surprised when I rose from bed with nary ache nor pain.

After returning to New Freedom on a Saturday evening, I rested a day and then ran on Monday morning. I felt fine the following morning, so I ran again that day. On Wednesday morning, though, when I attempted to get up, pain flattened me to the bed. Desperate for answers, I telephoned Suzanne, my physical therapist, and asked her to recommend a nearby medical facility where I might see a physician about my problem. I was fortunate, or so I thought, to see someone rather quickly. The physician, who seemed bumbling, ordered an x-ray of my pelvic region, reviewed the film, and told me to rest for a few days before resuming my runs.

I carried the x-ray with me when I saw Suzanne next. Blankly, she stared at the analysis: "Suspect mild calcific tendinosis of the right hip with well-circumscribed calcific density of the right greater trochanter. Hip joint spaces are maintained. Mild sclerosis of the pubic symphysis compatible with chronic osteitis pubis."

Before my appointment with Suzanne, I had read online articles about the condition. Osteitis pubis is an inflammation of the pubic symphysis and surrounding muscle insertions. It is an overuse injury caused by excessive running, kicking, and/or quick lateral movements. Instead of talking with me in clinical terms about the injury, Suzanne tactlessly blurted, "T. J., you're getting older, so you're developing arthritis in your right hip." I wondered whether she was going to suggest that I stop running.

Incensed, I found another physical therapist. The new person prescribed a sacroiliac belt that helped to stabilize my hips and alleviate groin pain when I ran. As she suggested, I iced my pelvic region as soon as I completed my runs to relieve inflammation. Several times daily, I performed fist squeezes, with moderate pressure, between my knees to restore pelvic alignment.

Although I continued to experience pain, I registered for the NCR Half Marathon, an out-and-back race on Saturday, November 24, 2018. David also signed up. Each weekend for six weeks, we drove about a half-hour to the NCR Trail and ran toward the race's turnaround spot, U-turned, and returned to the car. It was strategically parked with the front facing the Trail and the trunk backing an overgrown empty lot where the remains of a greenish ramshackle house stood. Hiding behind one of the back doors of the car, I could relieve myself by pulling my running skirt to the side or dropping my bike shorts without being seen.

Every Saturday, shortly after we hopped out of the car, David walked briskly from this spot. He started to run, and I remained behind, loosening my hamstrings by swinging each leg forward, balancing my hips by completing standing clamshells, and activating my gluteals by bending over the car's hood and doing donkey kicks. By the time I entered the Trail, he was not even a figure in the distance.

Although we usually covered the same number of miles, I returned to the car first because I ran faster than he did. He saw these training runs as endurance efforts while I saw them as mini races that would reveal how fast I could run during the actual half marathon.

While I waited for him, I stretched and wiped off the salt from my face and the sweat from my body with my *Finding Nemo* towel, which I bought years earlier to dry myself after swimming-lesson showers. Then I climbed inside the car, where its gray-tinted windows hid me from view as I changed into a dry sports bra and dry running top.

When David finished his run, he stretched and dried himself with a faded navy-blue bath towel discarded when it no longer fit the color scheme of a bathroom that I redecorated. Then, standing outside the car, he stripped off his top and changed into a dry shirt. Ravenously, he gobbled a sandwich of turkey, tomato, and spinach on whole-wheat bread jazzed with horse radish. I was envious. I had eaten only half of a bagel before the run. Although almost every article or book on long-run recovery encouraged immediate consumption of carbohydrates and protein after completion of such an effort, I waited at least two hours before I ate. Simply put, I was just not hungry. All I could stomach was a random sip of water and a few small salted pretzels as David drove us home.

Our half-marathon training runs bore fruit. By a smidgen, on race day, I completed my fastest 13.1-mile run in seven years. My time was 2:08:24. I bested the women in the 60-64 group and the 65-69 group as well as the only other woman in the 70-99 group. I finished faster than the men in the 70-99 group, which included David, who finished first in his group.

Four months later, I raced in the 2019 B and A Half Marathon. At packet pickup, I learned that the race was a Road-Runners-Club-of-America event. As such, it was the Maryland Half-Marathon Championship. Perhaps for this reason, the participants, their colorful tanks and t-shirts announced, represented a broader spectrum of runners than I expected. The competitors included not only members of nearby running clubs such as the Annapolis Striders and a US Navy team but also far-from-home groups such as the Korean Road Runners Club based in New Jersey and New York.

The B and A Half Marathon had not been in my plans. David registered, and he encouraged me to race also. My pelvic discomfort had diminished, so I did not have this problem as a convenient excuse. In all truth, I could have invoked burnout, which threatened to swallow me whole at this point. Fatigue fueled by a long-term sleep deficit translated into zero passion for the sport. My self-confidence had drooped. I worried about whether I could run as fast as I had during the recent NCR Half Marathon.

Alone, I meandered to the start line. David was nearby, but I ignored him. As the signal for the start interrupted conversations, I realized that I had forgotten to inhale Albuterol a half-hour earlier. Was this misstep a harbinger of ill fortune as the omens had been immediately before the 2016 Boston Marathon? Fortunately, the temperature was 64 degrees, and drizzle encapsulated us runners. I had no problem with breathing.

David and I had run the route three times before race day. During these practices, we descended and then ascended the half marathon's single hill. The distance each way was four-tenths of a mile, but during the actual race, we ran down six-tenths of a mile and ran up six-tenths of a mile. Gasping as I neared the top during the actual half marathon, I stopped running for about ten seconds and walked. When I looked up, my eyes met David's. He was on his way down the hill.

During the final mile, like other half-marathon finishers, I exited the B and A Trail at about 12.5 miles. Then I covered about half a mile on a long concrete sidewalk. Although curb cuts facilitated movement from block to block, I found such a finish bizarre. During my days of running with the Pacemakers, I had seen my fair share of runners missing curbs and landing splat on concrete sidewalks and rising with cuts and scrapes or worse, so I proceeded slowly and cautiously. I made a right turn into the parking lot, where the runners were to head, according to the published race information, straight ahead to the finish line. However, when I ran forward, a volunteer interceded and directed me to my right. When I protested, he said firmly, "You're supposed to run additional distance on the parking lot. Follow the cones."

At this point, I was exhausted and wanted to walk to the end. I needed to energize myself. Remembering the research about smiling, I fought to turn my lips upward, but they would not cooperate. Desperate, to a stranger on my left who appeared to be in her mid-twenties and who looked as whipped as I felt, I said, "I'll bet I can beat you to the finish." She giggled. We both sprinted as spectators applauded. I lost by one footfall.

As soon as I thought that I could in good conscience distract the race timer from entering finishers' hours, minutes, and seconds, I asked him, "How did I do?" Brusquely, he responded, "You finished." I stayed near him. I was not going to budge until

I received the information that I sought. After a few minutes, he looked at his computer screen. "Your time was 2:11:34," he said.

"Where did I finish in the group?"

"You're the only person in your division who's finished the race so far."

Nine minutes after I crossed the finish line, David came in. Chuckling as soon as he joined me, he said, "You looked like the poster child for guilt when I caught you walking up part of the hill." After he finished laughing, I said, "I'm miffed with you. We didn't run far enough down the hill when we practiced, so I wasn't prepared for that long uphill." Calmly, he countered, "We ran the published race route, but the runners were taken farther down the hill because the race was short at the beginning."

The day after the race, the sponsors published a statement about course adjustments. The lead vehicle skipped part of the course during the first mile. Distance was added at the midpoint and at the finish. While the hill extension was an unpleasant surprise, the added distance on the parking lot when I could smell the dirt-encrusted timing mat was a crueler cut.

Although I was first in my age group, I reverted to my former self, the self-recriminator. I was more than two minutes slower than I had been in the NCR Half Marathon. Then I rationalized my B and A time. I compared the routes. Because of the hill, the B and A course was tougher, I told myself. The weather during the B and A was 20 degrees warmer, and I was a cold-weather runner. My negative thoughts continued even after I learned that I ran 14 minutes faster than the second-place finisher in my group and 27 minutes faster than the third-place finisher. Both of these women were active members of running clubs and not occasional runners. I ran faster than the second- and third-place finishers in the 65-to-69 female group and faster than the third-place finisher in the 60-to-64 female group. These comparisons failed to puff me up. Then I resorted to self-talk, reminding myself that I should be thankful for the largesse that surrounded me every single second. I forgave myself for this temporary regression. I acknowledged that overcoming the need for external validation was a constant struggle. One race at a time. One run at a time.

Mistakes and Heat Exhaustion: Preparing for My Tenth Marathon

Coach Buddy agreed to prepare a training schedule for me for the October 6, 2019, Wineglass Marathon, which began in Bath, New York, and ended in Corning, New York. He invited me to share my progress toward this marathon on *Running Around Baltimore*, a podcast. During the first episode in which I participated, I summarized my running history and provided an overview of my target marathon. Thereafter, I updated listeners about my training during "Coach's Corner," a segment during which Coach Buddy shared general running tips and provided on-air advice to another runner, the podcast's host who was himself preparing for a fall marathon, and to me.

During the next few months, I demonstrated that experience does not necessarily yield wisdom. In an email, I informed Coach Buddy that I planned to run two half marathons before the Wineglass Marathon. He replied, "If you do these races, you're going to be off script. I usually like runners to do a single half marathon. Midway, around nine or ten weeks into the marathon schedule."

I countered, "I'm still accustomed to 12- or 13-mile-long runs on Saturday or Sunday and three or four short runs during the week. I thought that a half marathon three and a half weeks into the schedule wouldn't be a stretch."

"The more you race, the more risk of injury."

"The more I compete, the more relaxed I should be on marathon day." (I do not know why I latched onto this false justification. I was consistently calm before and during races.)

"If you're determined to run this half marathon, I want you to treat it like a C race." In running lingo, a C race is one that is run for fun, a B effort is one that is run to prepare for a goal race, and an A run is the season's goal race.

He added, "Enjoy yourself. Run easily."

"That's going to be tough," I responded.

"Eyes on the prize. The prize is the full marathon."

His comments called to mind Margaret's long-ago urgings that I use some races as training runs during which I practiced hydration, fueling, and pacing. I had not been able to heed her suggestion in the past, but I vowed to follow it during the C and B races.

The first race that was off script occurred on June 30, 2019, in Savannah, New York, a small town about 280 miles north of New Freedom. This particular race, the Montezuma Half Marathon, appealed to me because I assumed, incorrectly, that the temperature and humidity there would be lower than in Pennsylvania. In this regard, the experience should have been dubbed Montezuma's revenge. No connection to digestive distress. Had I reviewed historical weather data carefully and been governed by this information, I would have stayed at home and lost my nonrefundable registration fee. But I showed up and ran.

All that I knew about this half marathon before I raced I learned from a few photographs on the race website and from an elevation table posted on *Map My Run* (an app that is used to plan and record running, walking, and biking routes). The out-and-back course appeared to be sharply rolling; the steep ups and downs were unlike the gently rolling terrain and long gradually rising hills on which I trained regularly. A week before the race, I began to fret. I emailed Coach Buddy, who graciously reviewed the route and pointed out commonalities with sections of a route near Loch Raven Reservoir that I had run countless times. Unfortunately, I had not trained there for over a year.

On Friday, June 28, two days before the race, David and I arrived in upstate New York. Usually, we reached a half-marathon location a day ahead of the event, but the destination was a little over five hours away. I did not want to be overly tired on race day. On Saturday morning, we drove onto the course and learned that a steep rise was included in the route. Also, we saw that some of the running surface was hardly ideal. A mile was on a road covered with freshly laid chunky gravel in irregular straight-edged shapes, some rough and some smooth but all foreshadowing possible ankle injuries. Next, we drove slightly downhill on twin gray-brown dirt paths, each about as wide as a compact-car tire, through a three-to-four-mile looped area that was an emerald-green mix of woods, marshes, and grasslands. After we completed the loop, David's car bounced over the mile of chunky gravel again when we exited this area of the race course.

An hour later, we picked up my race bib and schwag bag containing a Buff and a glass, each of the latter emblazoned with the half-marathon name and an image of the race's bald-eagle mascot. David and I whined to the woman distributing the items about the course's difficulty. With a puzzled look on her face, she asked, "How did you get onto the island?" David replied, "Island? We didn't cross any water." She said, "The section with all the tall grass. There are gates that keep vehicles other than official trucks out." David responded, "The gates were open. So, we drove through. After a few minutes, we saw a truck ahead of us with two men who were putting up mile markers." Through good fortune, we deduced later, we had timed our exploration of the course during a narrow window when we could enter and leave the "island."

The woman told us that we must have driven over an elevated wooden bridge to reach this area, which was surrounded by the Seneca River and the Erie Canal. Neither David nor I remembered such a structure. I saw some bits and pieces of gleaming water peeking through twisted greenery but nothing that suggested that a river or canal was nearby. I reasoned that perhaps we had been beamed there through a transporter in much the way that Scotty of *Star Trek* beamed Captain Kirk and other crew members from and to the Starship Enterprise.

On Sunday morning, we arrived near the start of the race approximately 45 minutes before the half marathon was scheduled to begin. We parked near a visitors' center that had porcelain toilets and sinks with warm water. What luxury!

I decided to experiment. Fifteen minutes before the scheduled start, I primed myself. I had read an article that included advice about warming up before races up to the half-marathon distance by completing a burst of running at 5K speed for 45 to 60 seconds during a 10-to-20-minute period immediately prior to racing. This preparatory run opened blood vessels and activated enzymes in the muscles. The theory was that a runner would have enough time to recover before racing. As someone who struggled early on, I embraced anything I could do in advance to perform well from the start. After this burst, I performed my usual hip-high forward kicks, standing clamshells, and standing donkey kicks. Then I looked around for a place for a last-minute tinkle. I did not have enough time to stand in line for a porcelain toilet, so I hid behind the doors of David's car and behind the doors of the car parked next to us. The driver was a veteran runner and, to my amusement, had offered me the use of his doors as a second shield. I did not even have to ask. He knew the drill.

Instead of donning a water vest as I usually did, I planned to rely on water stops. I wanted to be prepared for all drinking options when I ran for the prize, my upcoming marathon, in October.

As I walked toward the start line, I went through my last-minute mental checklist. I anticipated gnats crawling up my nose or into my ear canals and mosquitoes biting my forearms and sprayed myself a bit too enthusiastically with insect repellent. Some of the stream, poorly directed, splashed into my eyes. Although my eyes burned, I stayed on task. I arranged the paper towels and the caffeinated gum that I had stuffed inside my sports bra. I carried no gels. A half bagel two hours before race time was sufficient nutrition. I looked down at my GPS watches—one on my left arm and another on my right arm. I had been wearing my GPS watch in addition to my GPS-music watch ever since David gave me the latter as a gift in 2018 for my 73rd birthday. I turned both on. Still haunting me was the 2016 Boston Marathon debacle when my GPS watch fell apart. For the first mile of the half marathon, tunes boomed through my wireless bone-conduction headphones, another gift from David. Suddenly, the music died. I did not stop to attempt to resuscitate the watch. Singing loudly and only slightly off key, a thirtyish African-American woman whose upbeat body language suggested glee met my music needs until I left her behind during the final three miles. Running karaoke!

At the start, the temperature was 72 degrees, and the humidity was around 90 percent. In deference to these conditions, I monitored my speed carefully. Despite exercising restraint, I ran the first mile faster than I planned. I slowed down. My objective was to run each mile in the neighborhood of 10:30. At the end of the second mile, I ran to the farthest and least crowded beverage table. After catching the eye of a volunteer, I clearly stated that I wanted water only. I formed a V at the cup's lip to direct the water into my mouth and swallowed slowly to achieve maximum absorption. I walked briskly on the right of the route because I still could not drink and run simultaneously. I tossed my cup into a trash receptacle after draining it. Swoosh! Two points! I repeated this process every two miles. A clean shot each time.

Midway, I became overheated. At a water stop, a short white-haired man with kind blue eyes and a gentle smile handed me a cup of water. As I accepted it, I said, "I need another cup so that I can throw it on my face." He offered, "Do you want me to douse you?" I replied, "Sure." He threw the water upward with such force that it went up my nose. I felt as though I were drowning. Coughing and sputtering, I learned a lesson at that moment—to refuse such help in the future.

Around the eighth mile, I looked ahead and saw the hill that David and I had seen during our reconnaissance. It evoked thoughts of Mount Everest. Maybe I should have recruited a Sherpa to accompany me. Its apex seemed to be hidden by diaphanous cotton-ball clouds. To expend as little energy as possible to reach the top, I blended yogging and race walking. Around mile ten, Mother Nature smiled; cool rain fell. Fickle, she changed her mind during the eleventh and twelfth miles. She frowned; headwinds slowed me. During the 13th mile, a tailwind propelled me, and I picked up the pace enough to sprint through the rest of the race. The finish-line timer read 2:17 when I crossed the mat. My average pace was 10:29 per mile—41 seconds slower per mile than my pace during the cooler B and A Half Marathon three months earlier but a hair faster than was my 10:30 objective.

Immediately after the race, I mingled with other runners. I joined a group of women who appeared to be in their late 30s and early 40s. One of them was livid because the course was so challenging. Bitterly, she proclaimed that she was "one and done" for this race. Like me, she had registered for the Wineglass Marathon. She confessed that she had run so slowly during the half marathon that she doubted her ability to run well for 26.2 miles. A few minutes into this conversation, I glanced to my right and saw the singing runner flit past me. I walked away from the group of women and ran off to introduce myself and to thank her for distracting me with her renditions of popular tunes. She giggled in response. As David and I waited for the half-marathon awards program to begin, a muscular twentyish man with tattoo-covered arms and legs and long sweat-drenched brown hair trotted up to me and startled me with a fist bump. Smiling, he said, "Thanks for getting me through the race. You were my inspiration." I had not noticed him as I ran. I was more memorable, I guessed, because I was one of only two African-American women, as far as I could tell, who participated in the half marathon.

When I checked the race results that evening in the hotel room, I learned only three people over 70 ran in the race. Another woman and I, both of us 73 years old, were the oldest participants of either gender. She finished an hour and four minutes after I crossed the line. A 72-year-old man was the only person of his gender in the 70-99 men's group. He came in 42 minutes after I finished. Maybe other people around my age had too much sense to run in such conditions and on such a course. When I looked at the overall gender numbers, I learned that I finished in the top 40 percent of 115 women. Not bad.

Seven weeks later, I toed the line at the Hellbender Half Marathon in Weiser State Forest in Bear Gap, Pennsylvania. The half marathon honored the state's official amphibian, the Eastern hellbender salamander. The animal was so named because these nine-to-sixteen-inch creatures, which secrete mucus through their skin when they feel imperiled, were said to look like demons from Hell.

Another bad move. The conditions during this half marathon were worse than those during the Montezuma Half Marathon. The temperature soared to 90 degrees, the sun blazed, and the humidity held steady at 90 percent. After I crossed the finish line, I wrung more water from my clothing than I had ever squeezed from my shorts or top after a race.

In addition to the weather, the course was a challenge. When I emailed the race director before I registered to inquire about an elevation map, he responded, "I don't have one. The route is flat and shaded." An alarm should have rung loudly. No map! Instead, he emailed me a photograph of the start, a section that was probably 100 feet long. When David and I checked out the area on our way home from the Montezuma Half Marathon, we saw that this specific bit of terrain matched the director's description. Unfortunately, the course covered close to 13 miles that were not captured in the snapshot and 12 miles that we did not check during our reconnaissance.

To me, when I ran the race, the full course did not sync with the race director's description. The Hellbender route seemed rolling rather than flat; around the midpoint, a "steepish" hill appeared. The vast majority of the course was indeed tree lined, as the director indicated, but the shade offered scant relief. I had assumed that "shaded" equaled increased coolness, even on a flaming-hot day. I was wrong.

My half-marathon objective was to practice marathon pace around 10:30 yet again. However, because of the heat, sun, and humidity, I was a little slower than I had planned. My finish time was 2:19. My pace was 10:38.

I was the oldest runner of either gender. I finished in the top 60 percent of all runners both male and female. I finished in the top 53 percent of all women runners. In my age group, I finished first. As usual, the competition in the 70-99 female group was minimal. A 70-year-old woman finished an hour and 35 minutes after I did. The weather took a heavy toll on her, I assumed.

Little about the Hellbender Half Marathon meshed with my upcoming marathon. The half marathon's soft surface, dirt and crumbled asphalt primarily, was unlike the firm asphalt highways and city streets on which I would run during the Wineglass Marathon. Also, by competing in this 13.1-mile race, I failed to adhere to my marathon-training plan. My schedule called for an 18-mile run on the day of the half marathon. After I crossed the finish line, I had planned to run five additional miles to make up the difference. I was too depleted to run the extra miles.

Four days after the half marathon, I was supposed to run 20 miles. The high that day in New Freedom was 93 degrees, and the low was 67. The humidity at its highest was in the 90s. In these conditions, I ran slowly for sixteen miles and then wilted.

My nutrition—the same blend of water, rice starch, beet powder, and beta alanine that I consumed during the 2018 Boston Marathon—failed me. Swaying back and forth and questioning my ability to walk home, I stopped and stood still time and time again.

Despite this setback, four days later, I attempted another 20-mile run, a violation of my training plan. I was supposed to drop down to 12 miles, but I wanted to run another 20 miler before I departed for an annual girls-only vacation with my sisters and my nieces. I ran only 18 miles.

This year, our destination was Las Vegas. While there, we gorged ourselves daily. They gambled; I was too risk averse to chase jackpots. The 100-degree-plus weather stopped me in my tracks whenever I ventured outside intending to run. On a dime, I turned around each time and retreated to the hotel's air-conditioned comfort. I peeked into the fitness center with its row upon row of burnished gun-metal treadmills, gleaming steel elliptical trainers, white weight machines, and the blackest-black iron free weights. Again and again, I changed my mind.

These icy confines were no more appealing than the blazing outdoors.

Two days after I returned from Las Vegas, I tried to run 20 miles again. Once more, I completed only 18 miles. I immediately emailed Coach Buddy to tell him about my difficulty covering this distance. He suggested that nutrition might be a major cause. He recommended a water-soluble powder popular among ultramarathoners that should meet my needs without upsetting my stomach. I tested the product initially during a 10-mile run. It provided enough carbohydrates. It did not wreak havoc with my digestive system. Eureka!

I relied on the powder again on what was supposed to be a 22-mile run on yet another blazing hot day. I began at my usual starting point near home, ran through the neighborhood, and reached the Trail after running three and a half miles. Then I ran south for 17 miles. Overcome by the heat, humidity, and unabated sun, I truncated the distance to 20.5 miles. I could not go on. As I stopped, a woman happened to be walking briskly toward me. I must have looked spent. She slowed and asked me, "Are you okay?"

"I'm fine," I lied.

"Are you sure?"

"I could use a bit of help with getting my cell phone out of the back pocket of my water vest. I can't seem to reach it."

After she gave me the phone, I thanked her—too profusely. In hindsight, I wondered why I had not just taken the water vest off. The phone would have been readily accessible had I done so. Maybe I thought then that I would continue to run after I made my call.

I tapped in David's cell-phone number. I asked him, "Can you drive down to the two-mile marker to pick me up?" He was in a parking lot that was two miles south on the Trail by foot. He had driven there earlier in the day and run from this location and then returned to his car. The plan was that I would run from home to his car in this lot. He replied, "You're not that far away. Why don't you walk here?" He responded in this fashion because getting to me by vehicle was not straightforward; he would have to drive about six circuitous miles on nearby roads to reach me. I had too much pride to beg. I hung up and plodded onward. After I lumbered for about a mile, I looked ahead. There David was. He looked as pooped as I imagined that I looked. I asked him, "How far did you run?" He said, "Fourteen miles. Seven miles north and then back to the car." Walking next to me on my left side, he reached his right hand out to take the water vest that I had removed after our brief telephone conversation.

I considered bailing from the Wineglass Marathon. I knew that I could finish the distance, but doubts about running well plagued me. Opting out would not be easy. I had been participating in the podcast with Coach Buddy and did not want to disappoint him or the *Running Around Baltimore* audience. Maybe I could claim to be injured. Prevarication was not one of my assets, so I decided to run, come what may.

Pragmatism: My Tenth Marathon

Cacophony! Jarring static emanated from the black plastic clock radio! Loud buzzing came from David's sports watch! The telephone jangled. David and I hopped out of bed. The time was 4:15 a.m.

The Wineglass Marathon began promptly at 8:15 a.m. David was registered for the Wineglass Half Marathon, which began at 7:30 a.m. We had agreed to leave our hotel room in Bath, New York, by 6:10 a.m. so that we could travel five minutes by car to a park in the downtown section of the city. There we would board one of a legion of yellow school buses transporting runners to the starts of their races.

We rose early so that we could tinkle time and time again and fully poop during this two-hour window. We drank coffee as soon as we arose. I chewed on a whole cranberry-nut bagel that I had brought from home and that David toasted in the hotel's breakfast area shortly after he got up. He devoured long-run cake (a homemade blend of black beans, chocolate, agave, and oat flour). Finally, we dressed in the running clothes that we had set out the night before. To save ourselves a step, we had showered immediately before we went to bed. In the morning, we smelled only like one another after a night of spooning.

Once we reached the park, David walked quickly to one of the buses lined up near the Bath Court House. The half marathoners would travel to the heart of Campbell, New York, for the start of their race. I waited in the car until 7:00 a.m. and then boarded a bus that took full marathoners to Bath's periphery for the start of the 26.2-mile race.

On this cloudy morning, the temperature was 51 degrees, and the humidity was 90 percent. Considering the soaring heat in which I had run for months, I luxuriated in these conditions.

Once I arrived at the start, I joined hundreds of other marathoners in a white tent. The racers who could not fit inside the tent or who simply preferred not to be inside stood or sat in a nearby building or milled around outside. At the eleventh hour, I left the tent and rushed to a porta-potty for my last tinkle. I turned on my two watches. When I was sure I could hear tunes coming through my wireless earphones, I looked at the signs the pacesetters held up. The 10:40 sign was the only one I saw that was close to my aspirational pace of 10:30. When I crossed the start line, I was a little behind this group, about 20 in number. When I caught up, I decided to run a little faster than these racers were moving. This decision would come back to bite me.

The first four or five miles of the course, gently rolling at this point, were on streets in Bath. Around the fifth mile, the route veered to the left and up a steep hill and then became rolling again. I was running in unknown territory. David and I thought that we had driven the marathon course months earlier when I was still in the process of deciding whether I would register. I had no idea where we drove at that time, but we had not been on this road. This point was reemphasized when, around mile fourteen, I stared at a hill that I had not seen during our reconnaissance. When I viewed the data on my GPS watch after the marathon, the elevation gain from the bottom to the top was close to 25 feet, and the distance was about a quarter of a mile. But it seemed like one of the Alps to me at the time. When I talked to David after the race about the difference between what my watch reflected and how formidable the hill seemed when I ran up it, he explained, "You thought that the incline was so tough because you didn't expect it. It's all about expectations. Because you were surprised, you magnified it."

I ran around 10:30 pace until I reached mile 18 when I began to tire and slowed down. Around this time, my GPS-music watch froze. I did not panic. In the past, it had stopped in the middle of several training runs, and it had stopped during the Montezuma Half Marathon. I had decided prior to the race that I would be willing to give up some time in exchange for upbeat tunes. I had practiced restarting the music watch while running, but I had to stop completely during the marathon when it died. Taking advantage of this brief break, I stretched my right hamstrings, which had begun to tighten. I checked my regular GPS watch. This stop cost me two minutes. Around this time, the 10:40 pace group, now perhaps half the original number, ran merrily by me. Some of them chatting. Others laughing. The pace-group leader encouraging them with a smile in her voice.

Around mile 22, I realized that unless I fainted on the course or became so injured that I could not move, I would be able to meet the 2021 Boston Marathon qualifying time for the 75-79 age group. I had shared this objective with no one, not even David, for fear of jinxing myself.

I decided not to push myself. There was little point, for I would start in the last group of runners at Hopkinton just as I had during my past Boston Marathons. When I saw the finish line in downtown Corning, which seemed to be at least a half mile away when it came into view, I picked up my pace and ran as fast as I could across the mat. My as-fast-as-I-could pace was probably around 8:00 per mile. Not much of a sprint.

After the race, I checked my watch. I had run almost a quarter of a mile more than the marathon distance. My lack of familiarity with the course and my subsequent inability to cut the tangents no doubt increased my distance as did my running to and from the sides of the route a few times so that I could slap the small hands of cheering children.

I finished the Wineglass Marathon, my tenth marathon in ten years, in a net time of 4:50:40, hardly my fastest marathon but fast enough for me to come in first of three women in the 70-99 age group. For Boston-Marathon registration purposes, I had close to 15 minutes to spare. The minimum qualifying time in 2021 for 75-79-year-old women would be 5:05.

By finishing the race, I remained in an exclusive club of women marathoners 70 years old or older—a group I had joined when I completed the 2016 Boston Marathon. According to *www.marastats.com* (*Marathon and Half Marathon Statistics, 2020*), only .2 percent of females who finished worldwide marathons in 2019 were 70 years of age or older. This rate translated into two of 1,000 women marathoners. As an African-American woman 70 years old or older, I belonged to an even more exclusive group of runners. Tony Reed, co-founder and executive director of the National Black Marathoners Association, estimates that, in 2019, US Black female marathoners in my age group constituted 0.00215 percent, or one in 46,512, of US marathon finishers. (His estimate is based on an analysis of eight US races from 2009 to 2019.)

A few days after the Wineglass Marathon, Coach Buddy reviewed my pacing. He emailed, "You really slowed down during the final quarter of the race. You need to work on building endurance in the future." I agreed although I knew that my giving up two minutes to restart my watch and to stretch my hamstrings was, in addition to my increasing fatigue, a major reason for my slowing pace. To him, I offered none of these excuses. He was right. I needed to improve my stamina.

I thanked Coach Buddy for helping me and for recommending the glycogen-replacement powder that I mixed with water and drank during the race. In a subsequent email to me, he floored me when he commented, "Don't be surprised if your body changes and the powder doesn't work during your next marathon." Yikes!

After this exchange with Coach Buddy, I reflected on my Wineglass-Marathon time.

To David, I proclaimed, "I know that I can run faster."

He replied, "People usually become slower as they age."

"Is the loss of speed a requirement for oldsters?"

"In most cases."

A week or so later, I emailed Coach Buddy to float the idea of my running in the NCR Half Marathon again; the race would occur in a few weeks. He thought that an expectation of a 9:45 pace was reasonable, given that my pace in the same race a year earlier had been 9:48. I decided that I could run faster than this pace, but I told neither Coach Buddy nor David about this belief. Each time I ventured out, I ran at tempo pace, around 9:25. I did neither slow runs nor speed work. During my weekend long run, I ran as fast as I could, even when doing so meant that I had to stop for ten or so seconds now and then. I thought that adrenaline on race day would keep me going nonstop.

As soon as I crossed the start line on race day, I morphed into an Amazon. When I participated in this race in 2017 and 2018, I ran the first few miles slowly. I thought that I should warm up and then increase my speed as the half marathon unfolded. This time around, though, from the jump, I attacked the course, an approach that was doable and had been highly possible during the two earlier versions of the race I had run because the first mile was almost totally downhill. Motivated by anger, I threw caution to the wind. A woman had implied that there was something fishy about my time the year before when I had come in first in my age group as I had during the previous year. In an email to me a day after the 2018 half marathon, she observed that there was no photo of me running that had been posted on the BRRC webpage. When I checked, I saw that she was correct. Quickly, I realized that the photos were only of runners in the BRRC half-marathon training program. I had not participated. I wondered whether this woman had looked for photos of every other BRRC member who had won an award. Why did my time matter to her? Was she competing with me even though she did not run? I was puzzled. When I mentioned her implication to David, he replied, "There are several photos of you running in the half marathon. I saw them." At that point, I reviewed all of the race photos—hundreds of them—on the general half-marathon page, and I found four of me. Gosh! My tummy looked huge.

As I dashed north and then south during the half marathon, I still seethed. I was determined to run faster than I had in the year during which my time was questioned. When I reached the half marathon's midpoint, my overall pace was 9:23 per mile. After I U-turned, fatigue slowed me a tad. My overall pace when I crossed the finish line was 9:33, 15 seconds per mile faster than my 9:48 pace the year before. I was astounded. I had run my second fastest half marathon of all time and my fastest in nine years.

When I emailed Coach Buddy about the race, he congratulated me on this result. He said, "I've found that my fastest times in shorter races have come within about ten weeks of a marathon as long as I maintained a base." Steadily, I had run after the Wineglass Marathon. Maybe my body responded as had his.

Then the coronavirus pandemic began. My next marathon, the Novo Nordisk New Jersey Marathon, was delayed from April 26, 2020, to November 15, 2020. I had been training for almost three months when the postponement was announced. I had finished an 18-mile run three days before I received an email about the change.

I opted to accept a refund in the form of a credit at an online running store rather than a transfer to the rescheduled marathon. Preparing for the new date meant that I would have to train through the summer. After enduring debilitating heat and humidity in summer 2019 when I prepared for the October 2019 Wineglass Marathon, I had vowed never to train again in such conditions.

Without the marathon hanging over my head, I had the luxury of dialing back my training. The day after I learned about the postponement, I skipped my usual Monday run. Rejuvenated a little after this brief rest, I covered four miles on my neighborhood's asphalt streets on Tuesday instead of my usual five miles. By design, I ran at a slower pace than I would have usually. When I ran on Wednesday, I opted for a six-mile out-and-back route on the Trail. That day I smiled at a little girl with lips the color of dark-red cherries and hair the color of milk chocolate. On a bike with noisy training wheels, she pedaled furiously behind me. When I reached a cross walk, I turned around to ensure that her parents were close enough to prevent her from crossing over to the distant side of the street. They were nearby and called out to her, "Wait for us!" Shortly thereafter, I said, "Hello" to a thirtyish man walking behind a balance-challenged tow-haired toddler who tripped and fell onto the Trail's soft-gravel surface a few times. I tried to pass a group of four women spread across the Trail who appeared to be oblivious to my footfalls. I pulled up the Buff that I wore around my neck for use as a face mask. Then I slowed, and as soon as I saw a narrow path with enough space to dash past them, I sped up, giving them a wide berth—not quite six feet of social distancing as recommended by medical professionals but as far away from them as I could manage. Coming toward me was a white-haired couple I saw often on the Trail. They waved and smiled. I waved and smiled back.

Without any races for which to train, I ran for the sheer joy of the sport and the accompanying physical-fitness and mental-health benefits. I hoped that my next marathon would be the 2021 Boston Marathon. If somehow I did not gain entry or the race did not occur because of the pandemic, I would run faithfully, nonetheless.

OH, HAPPY DAY! ANOTHER MORNING RUN

From March 2009 through March 2020, I had run a total of approximately 14,000 miles, excluding races; raced 583 miles; and competed in 53 races. I had run in ten marathons and qualified for the Boston Marathon eight times. Grateful!

I planned to run five miles this warm May morning. As my mind leaped from subject to subject, I listened to The Talking Heads' "Once in a Lifetime," one of my favorite songs by this acclaimed American New-Wave band. Edgy Afro-beat rhythms. Lyrics about the hollowness of the American Dream: "And you may find yourself / Behind the wheel of a large automobile / And you may find yourself in a beautiful house / With a beautiful wife / And you may ask yourself, well / How did I get here?"

I sauntered to the end of my driveway, turned right, and strolled uphill for a tenth of a mile. No boxer and no schnauzer this morning. I walked for another two-tenths of a mile and made a right turn. I looked to my left. Oh, no! A light-gray Great Dane was tied to a black metal post in the backyard of a beige colonial house that had recently been sold. The dog, a male I quickly discerned, stared benignly at me.

I looked upward. Starlings—chunky birds with black plumage, short tails, and pointed, yellow bills—swooped onto emerald pine trees. Goldfinches—tiny birds with yellow plumage and orange or yellow-brown legs and feet—landed on the branches of black-walnut trees. House sparrows—small birds with pale brown or gray feathers and with bright black, white, and brown markings—rested on the branches of blue spruces.

For an instant, I looked to my left. A robin redbreast nibbled at red berries on a nearby shrub. For a longer period, I looked to my right. In the back yard of a pale-gray colonial house, with the barest traces of lime-green moss creeping up its siding, were a hot-pink plastic tricycle and a royal-blue-rimmed trampoline. Light-yellow daffodils, blue-grape hyacinths, and pink peonies bordered the house. Dark-green fescue grass blanketed the lawn. Bright-yellow dandelions, like miniature starbursts, had broken through overnight. A blue jay—its crest erect and its blue, white, and black plumage resplendent—attempted to force its beak into the tiny holes of a red plastic feeder hanging from a six-foot-or-so black metal plant stand with a single hook that was probably placed there months ago to entice ruby-throated hummingbirds.

When I reached the crest where I began most of my runs, I switched from a brisk walk to a slow run. I pressed the start button on my GPS watch. In a few feet, the street dead ended. I turned right, crossed over the street, and ran facing oncoming traffic. As I gazed ahead, I stopped in my tracks. Clop, clop, clop, clop! Trotting toward me was a dark-brown high-stepping horse pulling a black enclosed Amish buggy. Seated inside was a brown-bearded man wearing a black broad-brimmed hat, a collarless white shirt, and a collarless black jacket. Gently, he held the reins between two fingers on each hand.

I dashed to the opposite side of the street, assuming that no auto or truck traffic was approaching because I felt no vibrations from the asphalt. I waved to the man. He smiled and nodded his head in response. I had run on these streets for almost five years. I had never seen such a sight. Without thinking, I U-turned and followed the buggy. I ran as fast as I could. It disappeared.

What would Mama think about me chasing a horse and buggy on foot?

Heading toward the Trail, I passed Gracie's lawn on my right. She pranced. She yipped, "Hi." She wagged her tail. I blew her a kiss.

I turned right at the stop sign where her street ended. Like an insatiable lover, gravity grabbed me and held me so tightly that I could barely breathe. Moaning softly, I yielded as we, as one, descended the steep hill to the flat surface below.

Acknowledgments

This memoir captures a decade of running during which I enhanced my fitness and learned much about myself. This journey was possible because of the support of my family and friends.

Family First

I am indebted always to Mary G. Bryan, my mother, who passed away in 2003, six years before I became a runner. Her strength and endurance continue to be standards to which I aspire.

I thank David Preston, my husband since 1980, and Bryan Preston, our son. David has been a runner since the early days of our marriage and has "crewed" for me during races and trained with me. Also, he has read multiple drafts of this memoir and offered suggestions. Bryan has, with good humor, sat through countless conversations about running and about this memoir.

I am indebted to Joseph Bryan, my father, who passed away in the mid-1970s. As someone who worked 365 days a year as a small businessman, he modeled the importance of hard work.

I thank my five sisters—Doris Tanner, Gloria Ragler, B. Patricia Bryan, Mary A. Bryan, and Myrtle E. B. Dorsey. (Especially I appreciate Doris's trip and Myrtle's trip to the 2011 Boston Marathon to cheer me on.) I am grateful for the support of my two nieces—Kimberly Bryan and Christine Collins Warren (and the encouragement of Anthony Warren, Christine's husband, and Austin Warren, their son).

Finally, I thank my running family. I have identified a few of these "relatives" in the memoir by name. Others know who they are. Without the support of this extended family, I would never have run so far, so well, and so often.

Friends Next

Life is often serendipity. By chance, I met Lynne Lamberg, a medical writer and editor, several years ago during a meeting of the Baltimore Women's Giving Circle. Since that time, she has become a friend. She has encouraged me to be brave—to write and to accept the risks that come with creation. She has read this manuscript many times and has recommended improvements. I am grateful.

I thank Buddy Weber, a coach certified by the Road Runners Club of America, and a friend. He generously reviewed the sections of my memoir on training and racing and suggested changes to enhance clarity.

ONE LAST THING

Thanks for reading *Saving Myself One Step at a Time: A Running Memoir*. If you have a minute to spare, I would appreciate your writing a short review on the page or site on which you discovered or bought the book. Reviews from readers like you make a huge difference in helping new readers find books similar to this one.

Made in United States
North Haven, CT
27 January 2022